"One day Grandpappy sassed Miss Polly White, and she told him that if he didn't behave hisself that she would put him in her pocket. Grandpappy was a big man, and I ask him how Miss Polly could do that. H⬛⬛⬛⬛⬛⬛⬛⬛⬛⬛⬛'d sell him, then p⬛⬛⬛⬛⬛⬛⬛⬛⬛⬛⬛⬛He never did sass M⬛⬛⬛⬛⬛⬛⬛⬛⬛

BRO

"Slavery was a ⬛⬛⬛⬛⬛⬛⬛⬛⬛⬛⬛⬛e kind we got, with nothing to live on, was bad. Two snakes full of poison. One lying with his head pointing north, the other with his head pointing south. Their names was slavery and freedom. The snake called slavery lay with his head pointed south, and the snake called freedom lay with his head pointed north. Both bit the nigger, and they was both bad."

PATSY MITCHNER

"Marster had four overseers on the place, and they drove us from sunup till sunset. Some of the women plowed barefooted most all the time and had to carry that row and keep up with the men, and then do their cooking at night. We hated to see the sun rise in slavery time, 'cause it meant another hard day. But then we was glad to see it go down."

HENRY JAMES TRENTHAM
—*from* BEFORE FREEDOM

BELINDA HURMENCE was born in Oklahoma, raised in Texas, and educated at the University of Texas and Columbia University; she is the author of award-winning books for young people. *Before Freedom* includes the two volumes of oral history— *Before Freedom, When I Just Can Remember* and *My Folks Don't Want Me to Talk About Slavery*—which Ms. Hurmence edited.

◆　◆　◆

BEFORE FREEDOM:

48 Oral Histories of Former North and South Carolina Slaves

Edited by
Belinda Hurmence

A MENTOR BOOK

MENTOR
Published by the Penguin Group
Penguin Books USA Inc., 375 Hudson Street,
New York, New York 10014, U.S.A.
Penguin Books Ltd, 27 Wrights Lane,
London W8 5TZ, England
Penguin Books Australia Ltd, Ringwood,
Victoria, Australia
Penguin Books Canada Ltd, 10 Alcorn Avenue,
Toronto, Ontario, Canada M4V 3B2
Penguin Books (N.Z.) Ltd, 182–190 Wairau Road,
Auckland 10, New Zealand

Penguin Books Ltd, Registered Offices:
Harmondsworth, Middlesex, England

This is an authorized reprint of a hardcover edition published by
John F. Blair, Publisher.

First Mentor Printing, June, 1990
10 9 8 7 6 5 4 3 2

♦   ♦   ♦

Contents

Introduction

SARAH DEBRO, ONCE A slave in North Carolina, put it bluntly: "My folks don't want me to talk about slavery. They's shame niggers ever was slaves."

Sarah's folks are not alone in their embarrassment. Many Americans, white and black, prefer to overlook Sarah's role in that infamous period of United States history. After all, "we" aren't the ones to blame for her enslavement. Why bring it up at this late date? Why talk about slavery?

The answer is *Sarah*. To ignore her life under slavery is to ignore black pioneering in the United States—and, in effect, to deny Sarah's humanity, as it was denied in slavery time. That is why Sarah must be allowed to speak for herself. That is why it is important for her to talk about slavery.

From the time the new republic came into being, Americans wrestled with the problem of Sarah. Her very existence mocked the validity of a government that guaranteed liberty and justice for the nation's people. One argument solemnly maintaned that Sarah was not a person, that she counted only as property; and the Bible was cited as proof that her master was entitled to dispose of his property as he saw fit.

The argument prevailed, for economic reasons, and a system of government grew up around Sarah that provided for her liability under the law but provided her with no protection under that same law. She could not vote. She could not marry. She could not even claim as hers the children she bore, for they too were the property of her master.

The system worked well enough that millions of slaves remained in bondage for 246 years in America. It worked poorly enough that increasingly restrictive Slave Codes had to be written to keep the human property under control. Slaves were legally forbidden to read and write. Slaves could not buy and sell merchandise. They could not own or fire guns, they could not ride horses without permission. No gambling, no liquor, no preaching or holding religious services or other meetings, no slandering a free white person, no insolence to a free white person—the list grew longer with each new Code.

Even so, the slaves persisted in behaving like human beings. The passions that drove their masters surged in these people of oppression: joy and sorrow, love and hatred, generosity and greed. They had dreams and hopes, and they were aware of their dreams and hopes in the way that all people are aware. The Code that governed them never succeeded in eradicating their humanity.

When Freedom came to blacks in 1865, hard times came too. Many former slaves lamented that their sufferings multiplied after the War between the States. At least in the old days there had been certainty of food, clothing, shelter. Now there was no certainty, and nobody would listen to their problems.

It was true that nobody wanted to listen. The defeated, smarting South was preoccupied with binding up its wounds. The victor, a stunned North, found itself struggling to cope with four million needy new citizens clamoring for jobs, education, some land of their own. North and South, so recently divided, discovered common ground in righteous indignation: the slaves had been set free; why weren't they properly appreciative? Their unseemly grievances tarnished America's image. If they wouldn't put their past behind them, they ought at least, for history's sake, to keep quiet about it.

In fact, it took little to silence the former slaves. Their own children were either bored with the old tales or shamed by them. And in any case, those who had lived through slavery were accustomed to going unheard, just as though they did not exist. Soon they actually would not exist, for they were growing old. Before long, everybody who had experienced bondage would be dead, forever silenced.

Amazingly enough, in the midst of the Great Depression of the 1930s, a government agency urged them to speak up, to tell what they remembered of life under slavery, before Freedom. The Federal Writers' Project, created in those hard times to provide work for jobless writers and researchers, initiated a program in which field workers were dispatched throughout the erstwhile slave states to interview those who had experienced slavery, wherever they might be found. More than two thousand former slaves participated in this remarkable undertaking. Of these, 176 were North Carolinians, 284 were South Carolinians.

Oral histories have become commonplace and the tape recorder has revolutionized interview techniques. In the 1930s, however, field workers had to copy out the answers in long hand, and then retype them. The interviews were gathered together and assigned an overall title, *Slave Narratives: A Folk History of Slavery in the U.S. from Interviews with Former Slaves*. Ten thousand pages of voices from the past were placed in storage in the Library of Congress.

Vivid voices they were, too, at last having their say about that murky time "before Freedom."

Sylvia Cannon, former slave of "Old Marse Bill Briggs," in Florence County, South Carolina: "At night the overseer would walk out to see could he catch any of us walking without a note, and to this day, I don't want to go nowhere without a paper."

Fannie Griffin, once the slave of Joe Beard in Columbia, South Carolina: "I think about my old mammy heap of times now and how I's seen her whipped, with the blood dripping off of her."

The concept of bondage has always fascinated free Americans. With slavery more than a century behind us, and beyond the recollection of any living person, the fascination still persists. Perhaps the invisible ties that bind us one to another evoke a dread empathy with the physically enslaved. Scholars, researchers and writers have always felt the tug of emotions adherent to the *Slave Narratives*.

They have also felt overwhelmed by the material. For one thing, there is so much of it. For another, it is so uneven, sometimes bursting with bitterness, sometimes sweetly nostalgic in tone. Some of the ex-slaves were more articulate than others. The expertise of the field workers in committing personalities to paper varied greatly.

The sheer volume of the *Narratives* can be intimidating, and the collection remained virtually untouched for years. In time, the Library microfilmed the entire ten thousand pages to make the work more accessible. In more time, facsimile pages came to be published in multivolume editions.

Some years ago, in gathering background material for a novel I was then writing, I chanced upon the *Slave Narratives*. I too found the bulk of them daunting, but I saw at once the treasure that lay in this unwieldy collection. The *Narratives* resounded with an authenticity I had not encountered before in any prose dealing with slavery. It took me two years to read through the collection, and I ended up not only with an altered view of slavery, but also with an altered focus on what I wanted to write. I abandoned my novel and instead wrote two others, based on notes taken from *Slave Narratives*.

The powerful raw testimonies in the *Narratives* convinced me that they should be made available to casual readers as well as to scholars and historians. So I came to edit a selection, first from the North Carolina interviews, *My Folks Don't Want Me to Talk About Slavery,* and later, a companion volume featuring the South Carolina accounts, *Before Freedom, When I Just Can Remember*. The present edition combines the selections from the two states. In it, the reader may observe a certain uniformity of treatment from one state to another—work quotas, food rationing, the system of punishments. Popular magazines of the time devoted many articles to the topic of efficient slave management. Yet over and over, despite the deadening effect of this human bookkeeping, the live voice of the individual slave speaks out.

A reader of this volume may find it puzzling that some slaves of the Carolinas actually defend their servitude, as North Carolina's Mary Anderson does: "I think slavery was a mighty good thing for Mother, Father, me, and the other members of the family. . . ." Such a statement is almost incomprehensible to students educated after the civil rights advances of the 1960s, but the reader needs to keep in mind that these oral histories were collected half a century ago, in a time of depression and deep poverty for many whites and most blacks. The entire nation looked backward with nostalgia during the 1930s. To an aging, destitute black person, bondage may well have seemed less onerous in retrospect, particularly when compared with memories of an easygoing master, a full stomach, the energy of childhood.

It is also useful to remember that Freedom, following the Civil War, brought virtually no improvement in the lives of the liberated. The former slaves knew themselves to be free—but they also recognized their powerlessness. Reconstruction had quickly shattered their embryonic political aspirations. They had felt safer—they had undoubtedly *lived* safer—in the fiefdom of their former masters. Uneducated and ignorant of the world outside the plantation, oppressed by the law, threatened by night riders and Klansmen, few could see Freedom as a condition to be cherished.

And little support came from their liberators, the victors in the recent hostilities. The war-weary Yankees had lost interest in the high principle for which they had fought. Like their southern counterparts, they directed all their efforts toward rebuilding the strained economy, and left the new citizens to endure Freedom much as they had endured slavery. Field hands who had been exploited as slaves were ripe for exploitation as sharecroppers. Women trained as house slaves continued cooking and cleaning by day and by night took in washing, merely to subsist. A century would pass before the 1960s appreciably improved their opportunities.

The reader should also bear in mind the climate in which these interviews took place. The former slaves were responding to white questioners. By lifelong habit, they had learned to say what they believed the one in authority wished to hear. They used "jaw sense," as the adage held in time of slavery. The more outspoken individuals would most likely have fled the plantation at the time these interviews were collected, just as those early militants, the runaway slaves, did before Freedom. In this sense we may view the *Narratives* as somewhat weighted.

Taken as they come, however, the folk histories of America's former slaves ring true. The very artlessness of the ex-slaves brings authenticity to their words. The same can almost be said of the interviewers, for few of that small army of field workers had been formally schooled to the task given them. They were supplied with a list of questions to ask, instructed to write down the answers as nearly verbatim as possible, and by and large that is what they did. The result is a remarkably eloquent prose.

Choosing a reasonable sampling to represent the Carolinas from *Slave Narratives* at first appeared a hopeless task. Nearly every individual expressed some special viewpoint that I felt reluctant to omit. I finally made an arbitrary selection on the basis of the narrator's age, so that only records of those slaves who were about ten years of age or older at the time Freedom came are here included. Recollections of younger individuals are more likely to be based on hearsay, and the intent of the selection is to render accounts of actual experience or observation. Cutting was needed, in some instances, to eliminate hearsay, and I also made minor cuts of material either repeated or implied elsewhere in the same interview. Bracketed material within the text represents editorial comment or explanation.

I have not corrected the grammar of *Slave Narratives*, since the reader will surely appreciate that errors are to be expected from unlettered persons. I did correct certain misspellings used by the interviewers to register dialect, because they seemed to me excessive and hampered readability. I also rearranged the order of some passages, particularly in the longer narratives. My aim in so doing has been to impose a chronology upon the account, never to alter the speaker's style or meaning. I am responsible for editing the *Narratives* here presented, but all the words of those narratives are the ex-slaves' own.

—Belinda Hurmence

♦ ♦ ♦

My Folks Don't Want Me to Talk About Slavery
Twenty-one Oral Histories of Former North Carolina Slaves

For my parents
Eula and Warren Watson

Contents

◆　◆　◆

Ann Parker

*Age 103 (?) when interviewed in
the Wake County Home, Raleigh, N.C.,
by Mary A. Hicks*

I RECKON THAT I IS a hundred and three or a hundred and four years old. I was a woman grown at the end of the war.

I ain't had no daddy, 'cause queens don't marry, and my mammy, Junny, was a queen in Africa. They kidnaps her and steals her away from her throne and fetches her here to Wake County in slavery.

We belonged to Mr. Abner Parker, who lived near Raleigh, and he had maybe a hundred slaves and a whole heap of land. I ain't never liked him much, 'cause we had to work hard and we ain't got much to eat. He ain't allowed us no fun, but we did have some, spite of him.

We used to get by the pattyrollers and go to the neighboring plantations, where we'd sing and talk and maybe dance. I know once, though, that we was in a barn on Mr. Liles's place when the pattyrollers comed. All that could get out scatted, but the ones that got catched got a whupping.

I got several whupping for this, that, and t'other; but I 'spects that I needed them. Anyhow, we was raised right; we warn't allowed to sass nobody, and we old ones still knows that we is got to be polite to you white ladies.

Daughter, did I tell you about my mammy being a queen? Yes, she was a queen, and when she told them niggers that she was, they bowed down to her. She told not to tell it, and they don't tell, but when they is out of sight of the white folkses, they bows down to her and does what she says.

A few days before the surrender, Mammy, who am also a witch, says to them that she sees it in the coffee grounds that they am going to be free, so all of us packs up and gets out.

We got along pretty good after the war, and on till lately. After I gets too old to work, I sets on the post office steps and begs. I got a good pile of money too, but somebody done stole it, and now I's here in the County Home.

I fell and broke my arm some time ago, 'cause my right side am dead, and I tries to crawl off'n the bed. When I gets back from the hospital, they ties me in this chair to keep me from falling out, but I want to get a-loose. The nigger boy what helps me up and down ain't raised like I was; he fusses and he ain't got the manners what he ought to have.

Bob Jones

*Age 86 when interviewed August 17, 1937
at the County Home, Raleigh, N.C.,
by Mary A. Hicks*

I WAS BORNED IN Warren County, on the plantation belonging to Mister Bogie Rudd. My mammy
was Frankie. My pappy was named Harry Jones.
Him and my oldest brother, Burton, belonged to a
Mister Jones there in the neighborhood.

Marster Bogie and young Marster Joe was nice as
they could be, but Miss Betsy was crabbed and hard
to get along with. She whupped the servants what
done the housework, and she fussed so bad that she
mighty nigh run all us crazy. It was her what sold
my Aunt Sissy Ann, and it was her what whupped
my sister Mary so bad. There warn't but six of us
slaves, but them six run a race to see who can stay
out of her sight.

Young Marster Joe was one of the first to go to
the war, and I wanted to go with him, but I being
only fourteen, they decided to send Sidney instead.
I hated that, 'cause I surely wanted to go.

We never seed Marse Joe but twice after he left,
the time when his daddy was buried, and when they
brung his body home from the war. One day about
seven or eight Yankees comed around our place
looking for Reb scouts, they said, but they ain't find
none, so they goes on about their business. The

3

next day a few of our soldiers brings Marse Joe's body home from the war.

I don't remember where he was killed, but he had been dead so long that he had turned dark, and Sambo, a little nigger, says to me, "I thought, Bob, that I'd turn white when I went to heaven, but it appears to me like the white folkses am going to turn black."

We buried young Marse Joe under the trees in the family burying ground, and we niggers sung "Swing Low, Sweet Chariot," and "Nearer My God to Thee" and some others. The old missus was right nice to everybody that day, and she let the young missus take charge of all the business from that time.

We stayed on the Rudd plantation for two years after the war, then we moves to Method, where I met Edna Crowder. We courted for several months and at last I just puts my arm around her waist and I asks her to have me. She ain't got no mammy to ask, so she kisses me and tells me that she will.

During the course of our married life we had five chilluns, but only one of them lived to be named, that was Hyacinth, and he died before he was a month old.

Edna died too, six years ago, and left me to the mercies of the world. All my brothers and sisters dead, my parents dead, my chilluns dead, and my wife dead, but I has got a niece.

Till lately I been living at the Wake County Home, but my niece what lives on Person Street says that if'n I can get the pension that she can afford to let me stay to her home. I hope I does, 'cause I don't want to go back to the County Home.

◆ ◆ ◆

Henry James Trentham

*Age 92 when interviewed at
Route #2, Raleigh, N.C.,
by T. Pat Matthews*

IWAS BORN ON a plantation near Camden, North Carolina. I belonged to Dr. Trentham, and my missus was named Elizabeth. My father was named James Trentham, and Mother was named Lorie. I had two brothers and one sister. We all belonged to Mr. Trentham.

Marster's plantation was a awful big plantation with about four hundred slaves on it. It was a short distance from the Wateree River. Marster lived in a large two-story house with about twelve rooms in it. We called it the plantation house. Marster and Missus rode around in a carriage drawn by two horses and driven by a driver. They had four women to work in the house as cooks, maids, and the like.

The slave houses looked like a small town, and there was grist mills for corn, cotton gin, shoe shops, tanning yards, and lots of looms for weaving cloth. Most of the slaves cooked at their own houses, that they called shacks. They was give a'lowance of rations every week. The rations was tolerably good, just about like people eat now. Our marster looked after us when we got sick.

Marster had four overseers on the place, and they drove us from sunup till sunset. Some of the women plowed barefooted most all the time, and had to carry that row and keep up with the men, and then do their cooking at night. We hated to see the sun rise in slavery time, 'cause it meant another hard day; but then we was glad to see it go down.

The cornshuckings was a great time. Marster give good liquor to everybody then. When anybody shucked a red ear, he got a extra drink of whiskey. We had big suppers then, and a good time at cornshuckings. After the shucking, at night, there would be a wrestling match to see who was best on the plantation. We got a week holiday at Christmas. Then was the time shoes was give to the slaves, and the good times generally lasted a week. At lay-by time was another big time. That was about the Fourth of July. They give a big dinner, and everybody et all the barbecue and cake they wanted.

There was a church on the plantation, and both white and black went to preaching there. There was Sunday school there, too. The preacher told us to obey our missus and marster. He told us we must be obedient to them. Yes sir, that's what he told us. They would not allow slaves no books, and I can't read and write. I did not get any learning.

No hunting was allowed a slave, if no white man was with him, and they was not allowed to carry guns.

There was a jail on the place for to put slaves in, and in the jail there was a place to put your hands in, called stocks. Slaves was put there for punishment. I seed lots of slaves whupped by the overseers. The pattyrollers come round ever now and then, and if you was off the plantation and had no pass, they tore you up with the lash. Some of the slaves run away. When they was caught, they was whupped and put in the stocks in the jail. Some of the slaves that run away never did come back. The overseers told us they got killed, reason they never come back.

When a slave died, there was only a few to go to the burying. They didn't have time to go, they was so busy working. The slaves was buried in plain wood boxes which was made by slave men on the plantation.

I saw slaves sold at Camden. Marster carried some slaves there and put them on the auction block and sold them. I was carried, but I was not sold. I went with the old doctor. I was his pet. They carried slaves away from the plantation in chains. They carried five or six at a time. If a nigger didn't suit him, he sold him. Missus didn't like for him to beat them so much, nohow.

I married Ella Davis thirty-one years ago in South Carolina, near Camden. We had twelve chilluns, six boys and six girls.

Slavery was pretty rough, and I am glad it is all over.

Elias Thomas

*Age 84 when interviewed August 6, 1937
at 521 Cannon Avenue, Raleigh, N.C.,
by T. Pat Matthews*

IT TOOK A SMART nigger to know who his father was in slavery time. I don't know my father's name, but my mother was named Phillis Thomas. I was born in Chatham County on a plantation near Moncure, February, 1853. My marster was named Baxter Thomas, and Missus was named Katie. She was his wife. I can just remember my mother. I was about four or five years old when she died.

My marster's plantation was first the Thomas place. There was about two hundred acres in it, with about one hundred acres cleared land. He had six slaves on it.

When I was eight years old, he bought the Boylan place about two miles from his first home, and he moved there. There was about one thousand acres of land of it all, with about three hundred acres cleared for farming. On the Thomas place his house had six rooms; on the Boylan place the house had eight rooms. He brought in more slaves and took over all the slaves after John Boylan died.

John Boylan never married. He was a mighty hard man to get along with, and Marster Baxter Thomas was about the only one who could do anything with him when he had one of his mad spells.

8

They were no blood relation, but Marster got possession of his property when he died. It was fixed that way.

We called the slave houses quarters. They were arranged like streets about two hundred yards on the north side of the great house.

Our food was pretty good. Our white folks used slaves, especially the children, as they did themselves about eating. We all had the same kind of food. All had plenty of clothes but only one pair of shoes a year. People went barefooted a lot then, more than they do now. We had good places to sleep, straw mattresses and chicken feather beds, and feather bolsters. A bolster reached clear across the head of the bed.

We worked from sun to sun, with one hour and a half to rest at noon or dinner time. I was so small I did not do much heavy work. I chopped corn and cotton mostly. The old slaves had patches they tended, and sold what they made and had the money it brought. Everybody eat out of the big garden, both white and black alike. Old Missus wouldn't allow us to eat rabbits, but she let us catch and eat possums. Missus didn't have any use for a rabbit.

Sometimes we caught fish with hooks in Haw River, Deep River, and the Cape Fear, and when it was a dry time and the water got low, we caught fish in seines.

My marster only had two children, both boys, Fred and John. John was about my age, and Fred was about two years older. They are both dead. My marster never had any overseer; he made boss men out of his oldest slaves.

We thought well of the poor white neighbors. We colored children took them as regular playmates. Marster's boys played with them too, and Marster gave them all the work he could. He hired both men and women of the poor white class to work on the plantation. We all worked together. We had a good time. We worked and sang together and everybody seemed happy. In harvest time, a lot of help was hired, and such laughing, working, and singing. Just a good time in general. We sang the songs "Crossing over Jordan," and "Bound for the Promised Land."

I never saw a jail for slaves, but I have seen slaves whipped. I saw Crayton Abernathy, a overseer, whip a woman in the cotton patch on Doc Smith's farm, a mile from our plantation. I also saw old man William Crump, a owner, whip a man and some children. He waited till Sunday morning to whip his slaves. He would get ready to go to church, have his horse hitched up to the buggy, and then call his slaves out and whip them before he left for church. He generally whipped about five children every Sunday morning.

We had prayer meetings on the plantation about once or twice a week. We went to the white folks' church on Sunday. We went to both the Methodist and Presbyterian. The preacher told us to obey our marsters. I remember the baptizings. They baptized in Shattucks Creek and Haw River. I saw a lot of colored folks baptized.

No books were allowed to slaves in slavery time. I never went to school a minute in my life. I cannot read and write.

I do not remember any slaves running away from our plantation, but they ran away from old man Crump's and Richard Faucette's plantations near our plantation. Jacob Faucette ran away from Faucette and Tom Crump ran away from old man

Crump. They ran away to keep from getting a whipping.

Colored folks are afraid of bears, so one of the slaves who saw Tom Crump at night told him he saw a bear in the woods where he was staying. Tom was so scared he came home next morning and took his whipping. Both came home on account of that bear business, and both were whipped.

I remember the Yankees. I will remember seeing them till I die. I will never forget it. I thought it was the last of me. The white folks had told me the Yankees would kill me or carry me off, so I thought when I saw them coming it was the last of me. I hid in the woods while they were there. They tore up some things, but they did not do much damage. They camped from Holly Springs to Avant's Ferry on Cape Fear River. William Cross's plantation was about half the distance. The camp was about thirty miles long. General Logan, who was an old man, was in charge.

I married Martha Sears when I was twenty-three years old. I married in Raleigh. My wife died in 1912. We had fourteen children, five are living now.

When the war closed, I stayed on eight years with my marster. I then went to the N.C. State Hospital for the Insane. I stayed there twenty-eight years. That's where I learned to talk like a white man.

◆ ◆ ◆

Mary Barbour

Age 81 when interviewed at
801 S. Bloodworth Street, Raleigh, N.C.,
by Mary A. Hicks

I RECKON THAT I was borned in McDowell County, because that's where my mammy, Edith, lived. She belonged to Mr. Jefferson Mitchel there, and my pappy belonged to a Mr. Jordan in Avery County, so he said.

Before the war, I don't know nothing much 'cept that we lived on a big plantation and that my mammy worked hard, but was treated pretty good. We had our little log cabin off to one side, and my mammy had sixteen chilluns. Fast as they got three years old, the marster sold them till we last four that she had with her during the war. I was the oldest of these four; then there was Henry and then the twins, Liza and Charlie.

One of the first things that I remembers was my pappy waking me up in the middle of the night, dressing me in the dark, all the time telling me to keep quiet. One of the twins hollered some, and Pappy put his hand over its mouth to keep it quiet.

After we was dressed, he went outside and peeped around for a minute, then he comed back and got us. We snook out of the house and along the woods path, Pappy toting one of the twins and holding me by the hand and Mammy carrying the other two.

I reckons that I will always remember that walk, with the bushes slapping my legs, the wind sighing in the trees, and the hoot owls and whippoorwills hollering at each other from the big trees. I was half asleep and scared stiff, but in a little while we pass the plum thicket and there am the mules and wagon. There am the quilt in the bottom of the wagon, and on this they lays we younguns. And Pappy and Mammy gets on the board across the front and drives off down the road.

I was sleepy, but I was scared too, so as we rides along, I listens to Pappy and Mammy talk. Pappy was telling Mammy about the Yankees coming to their plantation, burning the corn cribs, the smokehouses, and destroying everything. He says right low that they done took Marster Jordan to the rip raps down nigh Norfolk, and that he stole the mules and wagon and escaped.

We was scared of the Yankees to start with, but the more we thinks about us running away from our marsters, the scareder we gets of the Rebs. Anyhow, Pappy says that we is going to join the Yankees.

We travels all night and hid in the woods all day for a long time, but after awhile we gets to Doctor Dillard's place, in Chowan County. I reckons that we stays there several days.

The Yankees has tooked this place, so we stops over, and has a heap of fun dancing and such while we am there. The Yankees tells Pappy to head for New Bern and that he will be took care of there, so to New Bern we goes.

When we gets to New Bern, the Yankees takes the mules and wagon, they tells Pappy something, and he puts us on a long white boat named *Ocean Waves*, and to Roanoke we goes.

Later, I learns that most of the reffes [refugees] is

put in James City, nigh New Bern, but there am a pretty good crowd on Roanoke.

After a few days there, the *Ocean Waves* comes back and takes all over to New Bern. My pappy was a shoemaker, so he makes Yankee boots, and we gets along pretty good.

I was raised in New Bern, and I lived there till forty years ago, when me and my husband moved to Raleigh; and though he's been dead a long time, I has lived here ever since; and even if I is eighty-one years old, I can still outwork my daughter and the rest of these young niggers.

◆ ◆ ◆

Hannah Crasson

Age 84 when interviewed
by T. Pat Matthews

I WAS BORN ON John William Walton's plantation
four miles from Garner and thirteen miles from
Raleigh, North Carolina, in the county of Wake. I
am eighty-four years old the second day of this last
gone March. I belonged to Mr. John William Walton in slavery time. My missus was named Miss
Martha.

My father was named Frank Walton. My mother
was named Flora Walton. Grandma was 104 years
when she died. She died down at the old plantation.
Our great grandmother was named Granny Flora.
They stole her from Africa with a red pocket handkerchief. Old man John William got my great grandmother. The people in New England got scared of
we niggers. They were afraid we would rise against
them and they pushed us on down South. Lord,
why didn't they let us stay where we was, they
never wouldn't have been so many half-white niggers, but the old marster was to blame for that.

Our marster would not sell his slaves. He give
them to his children when they married off, though.
One of our master's daughters was cruel. Sometimes she would go out and rare on us, but Old
Marster didn't want us whupped. The old boss man

was good to us. I was talking about him the other night. He didn't whup us, and he said he didn't want nobody else to whup us. It is just like I tell you; he was never cruel to us.

Mr. Bell Allen owned slaves too. He had a-plenty of niggers. His plantation was five miles from ours. We went to church at the white folks' church. When Mr. Bell Allen seed us coming, he would say, "Yonder comes John Walton's free niggers."

The white folks did not allow us to have nothing to do with books. You better not be found trying to learn to read. Our marster was harder down on that than anything else. You better not be catched with a book. They read the Bible and told us to obey our marster, for the Bible said obey your marster.

We had a-plenty to eat, we sure did, plenty to eat. We had nice houses to live in, too. Grandma had a large room to live in, and we had one to live in. Daddy stayed at home with Mother. They worked their patches by moonlight, and worked for the white folks in the daytime. They sold what they made. Marster bought it and paid for it. He made a barrel of rice every year, my daddy did.

There was about twenty-four slaves on the place. My grandmother and mother wove our clothes. They were called homespun. They made the shoes on the plantation, too. We had a corn mill and a flour mill on the plantation. They had brandy made on the plantation, and the marster give all his slaves some for their own uses.

I swept yards, churned, fed the chickens. In the evening, I would go with my missus a-fishing. We eat collards, peas, corn bread, milk, and rice. We got biscuit and butter twice a week. I thought that the best things I ever ate was butter spread on biscuit. They gave us Christmas and other holidays.

Then they, the men, would go to see their wives. Some of the men's wives belong to other marsters on other plantations. We had cornshuckings at night, and candy-pullings. Sometimes we had quiltings and dances.

One of the slaves, my aunt, she was a royal slave. She could dance all over the place with a tumbler of water on her head, without spilling it. She sure could tote herself. I always loved to see her come to church. She sure could tote herself.

I remember the day the war commenced. My marster called my father and my two uncles, Handy and Hyman, our marster called them. They had started back to the field to work in the afternoon. He said, "Come here, boys," that was our young marster, Ben Walton, says, "Come here, boys. I got something to tell you." Uncle Hyman said, "I can't. I got to go to work." He said, "Come here and set down, I got something to tell you."

The niggers went to him and set down. He told them, "There is a war commenced between the North and the South. If the North whups, you will be as free a man as I is. If the South whups, you will be a slave all your days."

Mr. Joe Walton said when he went to war that they could eat breakfast at home, go and whup the North, and be back for dinner. He went away, and it was four long years before he come back to dinner. The table was sure set a long time for him. A lot of the white folks said they wouldn't be much war, they could whup them so easy. Many of them never did come back to dinner.

I was afraid of the Yankees, because Missus had told us the Yankees were going to kill every nigger in the South. I hung to my mammy when they come through. The first band of music I ever heard play, the Yankees was playing it. They were playing a song, "I am tired of seeing the homespun dresses the Southern women wear."

I was not married till after the surrender. I did not dress the finest in the world, but I had nice clothes. My wedding dress was made of cream silk, made princess with pink and cream bows. I wore a pair of morocco store-bought shoes. My husband was dressed in a store-bought suit of clothes, the coat was made pigeon-tail. He had on a velvet vest and a white collar and tie. Somebody stole the vest after that.

◆ ◆ ◆

Isaac Johnson

*Age 82 when interviewed in
Lillington, North Carolina,
Route #1, Harnett County,
by T. Pat Matthews*

I WAS TEN YEARS old when the Yankees come through. I was born February 12, 1855.

I belonged to Jack Johnson. My missus' name was Nancy. My father was Bunch Matthews; he belonged to old man Drew Matthews, a slave owner. My mother was named Tilla Johnson. She belonged to Jack Johnson, my marster. The plantation was near Lillington, on the north side of the Cape Fear River, and ran down to near the Lillington Crossroads, one mile from the river.

I was too small to work. They had me to do little things like feeding the chickens and minding the table sometimes; but I was too small to work. They didn't let children work much in them days till they were thirteen or fourteen years old. We played base, cat, rolly hole, and a kind of baseball called 'round town. Marster would tell the children about Raw Head and Bloody Bones and other things to scare us. He would call us to the barn to get apples and run and hide, and we would have a time finding him. He give the one who found him a apple. Sometimes he didn't give the others no apple.

Jack Johnson, my marster, never had no children of his own. He had a boy with him by the name of

Stephen, a nephew of his, from one of his brothers.
Marster Jack had three brothers—Willis, Billy, and
Matthew. I don't remember any of his sisters.

There was about four thousand acres in the plantation and about twenty-five slaves. Marster would
not have an overseer. No sir, the slaves worked
very much as they pleased. He whupped a slave
now and then, but not much. I have seen him whup
them. He had some unruly niggers. Some of them
were part Indian, and mean. They all loved him,
though. I never saw a slave sold. He kept his slaves
together. He didn't want to get rid of any of them.
No slaves run away from Marster. They didn't have
any excuse to do so, because whites and colored
fared alike at Marster's. Marster loved his slaves,
and other white folks said he loved a nigger more
than he did white folks.

Our food was fixed up fine. It was fixed by a
regular cook, who didn't do anything but cook. We
had gardens, a-plenty of meat, a-plenty, and more
biscuit than a lot of white folks had. I can remember the biscuit.

The white folks didn't teach us to read and write.
I cannot read and write, but the white folks, only
about half, or less than half, could read and write
then. There were very few poor white folks who
could read and write.

We went to the white folks' church at Neill's
Creek, a missionary Baptist church. I remember the
baptizings at the Reuben Matthews millpond. Sometimes after a big meeting, they would baptize twenty-
four at one time.

Dr. John McNeill looked after us when we were
sick. We used a lot of herbs and things. Drank
sassafras tea and mullein tea. We also used sheep
tea for measles, you knows that. You know how it

was made. Called sheep pill tea. It sure would cure the measles. About all that would cure measles then. They were bad then. Worse than they is now.

We played during the Christmas holidays, and we got about two weeks Fourth of July and lay-by time, which was about the Fourth. We had great times at cornshuckings, logrollings, and cotton-pickings. We had dances. Marster allowed his slaves lots of freedom. My mother used to say he was better than other folks. Yes, she said her marster was better than other folks.

Old Marster loved his dram, and he gave it to all his slaves. It sold for ten cents a quart. He made brandy by the barrels, and at holidays all drank together and had a good time. I never saw any of them drunk. People wasn't mean when they were drinking then. It was so plentiful nobody noticed it much.

I saw Wheeler's Cavalry. They come through ahead of the Yankees. I saw colored people in the Yankee uniforms. They were blue and had brass buttons on them. The Yankees and Wheeler's Cavalry took everything they wanted, meat, chickens, and stock.

We stayed on with Marster after the war. I've never lived out of the state. We lived in the same place until Old Marster and Missus died. Then we lived with their relations right on and here. I am now on a place their heirs own.

Sarah Louise Augustus

*Age 80 when interviewed at
1424 Lane Street, Raleigh, N.C.,
by T. Pat Matthews*

I WAS BORN ON a plantation near Fayetteville, North Carolina, and I belonged to J.B. Smith. His wife was named Henrietta. He owned about thirty slaves. My father was named Romeo Harden, and my mother was named Alice Smith. The little cabin where I was born is still standing.

My first days of slavery was hard. I slept on a pallet on the floor of the cabin, and just as soon as I was able to work any at all I was put to milking cows.

Mr. George Lander had the first tombstone marble yard in Fayetteville, on Hay Street on the point of Flat Iron Place. I waited on the Landers part of the time.

I can remember when there was no hospital in Fayetteville. There was a little place near the depot where there was a board shanty where they operated on people. I stood outside once and saw the doctors take a man's leg off. Dr. McDuffy was the man who took the leg off. He lived on Hay Street near the silk mill.

When one of the white folks died, they sent slaves around to the homes of their friends and neighbors with a large sheet of paper with a piece of black

22

crepe pinned to the top of it. The friends would sign or make a cross mark on it. The funerals were held at the homes, and friends and neighbors stood on the porch and in the house while the services were going on. The bodies were carried to the grave after the services in a black hearse drawn by black horses. If they did not have black horses to draw the hearse, they went off and borrowed them. The colored people washed and shrouded the dead bodies. My grandmother was one who did this. She was called Black Mammy because she wet nursed so many white children. In slavery time, she nursed all babies hatched on her marster's plantation and kept it up after the war as long as she had children.

Grandfather was named Isaac Fuller. Mrs. Mary Ann Fuller, Kate Fuller, Mr. Will Fuller, who was a lawyer in Wall Street, New York, is some of their white folks. The Fullers were born in Fayetteville.

When a slave was no good, he was put on the auction block in Fayetteville and sold. The slave block stood in the center of the street, Fayetteville Street, where Ramsey and Gillespie streets came in near Cool Springs Street. The silk mill stood just below the slave market. I saw the silkworms that made the silk and saw them gather the cocoons and spin the silk.

They hung people in the middle of Ramsey Street. They put up a gallows and hung the men exactly at twelve o'clock. I ran away from the plantation once to go with some white children to see a man hung.

The only boats I remember on the Cape Fear was the *Governor Worth*, the *Hurt*, the *Iser*, and the *North State*. Oh! Lord yes, I remember the stagecoach. As many times as I run to carry the mail to them when they come by! They blew a horn before they got there and you had to be on time 'cause they could not wait. There was a stage each way each day, one up and one down.

The Yankees came through Fayetteville wearing large blue coats with capes on them. Lots of them were mounted, and there were thousands of foot soldiers. It took them several days to get through town. The Southern soldiers retreated, and then in a few hours the Yankees covered the town. They busted into the smokehouse at Marster's, took the meat, meal, and other provisions. Grandmother pled with the Yankees, but it did no good. They took all they wanted. They said if they had to come again they would take the babies from the cradles. They told us we were all free. The Negroes begun visiting each other in the cabins and became so excited they began to shout and pray. I thought they were all crazy.

We stayed right on with Marster. He had a town house and a big house on the plantation. I went to the town house to work, but Mother and Grandmother stayed on the plantation. My mother died there, and the white folks buried her. Father stayed right on and helped run the farm until he died.

I was thirty years old when I married. I was married in my missus' graduating dress. I was married in the white folks' church, to James Henry Harris. The white folks carried me there and gave me away. Miss Mary Smith gave me away. The wedding was attended mostly by white folks.

My husband was a fireman on the Cape Fear riverboats and a white man's Negro too. My husband was finally offered a job with a shipping concern in Delaware, and we moved there. After his death I married David Augustus and immediately came back to North Carolina and my white folks, and we have been here ever since.

Simuel Riddick

Age 95 when interviewed at
2205 Everette Avenue, Raleigh, N.C.,
by T. Pat Matthews

MY NAME IS SIMUEL Riddick. I was born the fourth day February, 1841. My owners, my white people, my old mistress wrote me a letter telling me my age. My mother was Nancy Riddick; she belonged to the Riddicks in the eastern part of the state. My father was named Elisha Riddick. My marster was named Elisha, and my mistress, Sarah Riddick. They had three daughters, Sarah, Christine, and Mary; one boy named Asbury Riddick.

I was born in Perquimans County, North Carolina, and I have lived in North Carolina all my life. We had good food, for Marster was a heavy farmer. There were about two hundred acres cleared on the plantation, and about twenty-five slaves. The great house was where Marster lived, and the quarters was where we lived. They were near the great house. I saw only one slave whupped. I had mighty fine white people, yes, mighty fine white people. They did not whup their slaves, but their son whupped my mother pretty bad, because she did not bale enough corn and turnips to feed the fattening hogs.

He was a rangtang. He loved his liquor, and he loved colored women. The old man never whupped anybody. Young Marster married in the Marmaduke

25

family, in Gates County. He sold one man who belonged to his wife, Mary. I never saw a slave sold.

I have seen lots of pattyrollers. They were my friends. I had friends among them, because I had a young missus they run with. That's why they let me alone. I went with her to cotton-pickings at night. They came, but they didn't touch me. My young missus married Dr. Perry from the same neighborhood in Perquimans County. Bill Simpson married her sister. He was from the same place. Watson White married the other one. He was from Perquimans.

There were no half-white children on Marster's plantation, and no mixups that ever came out to be a disgrace in any way. My white folks were fine people.

I remember Marster's brother's son Tommy going off to war. Marster's brother was named Willis Riddick. He never came back.

When the war broke out, I left my marster and went to Portsmouth, Virginia. General Miles captured me and put me in uniform. I waited on him as a body servant, a private in the U.S. Army. I stayed with him until General Lee surrendered. When Lee surrendered, I stayed in Washington with General Miles at the Willard Hotel and waited on him. I stayed there a long time. I was with General Miles at Fortress Monroe and stayed with him till he was in charge of North Carolina. He was a general, and had the 69th Irish Brigade. He also had the Bluecats and Greentorches.

I waited on him at the Abbeck House, Alexandria, Virginia, after the war. I stayed with the general a long time after the war. I didn't go with General Miles when he was ordered to the plains of

the West. I stayed on the Bureau here in Raleigh.
Dr. H.C. Wagel was in charge. After I left the
Bureau, I worked at the N.C. State College several
years, then I worked with the city at the city parks.
I never left the state after coming here with General
Miles.

I got a letter from my missus since I been in
Raleigh. She was a fine lady. She put fine clothes
on me. I was a foreman on the plantation and
looked after things in general. I had charge of everything at the lots and in the fields. They trusted
me.

I haven't anything to say against slavery. My old
folks put my clothes on me when I was a boy. They
gave me shoes and stockings and put them on me
when I was a little boy. I loved them, and I can't go
against them in anything. There were things I did
not like about slavery on some plantations, whupping
and selling parents and children from each other,
but I haven't much to say. I was treated good.

◆ ◆ ◆

Josephine Smith

Age 94 when interviewed at
1010 Mark Street, Raleigh, N.C.,
by Mary A. Hicks

I WAS BORNED IN Norfolk, Virginia, and I don't know who we belonged to, but I remembers the day we was put on the block at Richmond. I was just toddling around then, but me and my mammy brought a thousand dollars. My daddy, I reckon, belonged to somebody else, and we was just sold away from him just like the cow is sold away from the bull.

A preacher by the name of Maynard bought me and Mammy and carried us to Franklinton, where we lived till his daughter married Dr. John Leach of Johnston County; then I was give to her.

All my white folkses was good to me, and I reckon that I ain't got no cause for complaint. I ain't had much clothes, and I ain't had so much to eat, and a-many a whupping, but nobody ain't never been real bad to me.

I remembers seeing a heap of slave sales, with the niggers in chains, and the speculators selling and buying them off. I also remembers seeing a drove of slaves with nothing on but a rag betwixt their legs being galloped around before the buyers. About the worst thing that ever I seed, though, was a slave woman at Louisburg who had been sold off from her three-weeks-old baby, and was being marched to New Orleans.

She had walked till she was give out, and she was weak enough to fall in the middle of the road. She was chained with twenty or thirty other slaves, and they stopped to rest in the shade of a big oak while the speculators et their dinner. The slaves ain't having no dinner. As I pass by, this woman begs me in God's name for a drink of water, and I gives it to her. I ain't never be so sorry for nobody.

It was in the month of August, and the sun was bearing down hot when the slaves and their drivers leave the shade. They walk for a little piece, and this woman fall out. She dies there 'side of the road, and right there they buries her, cussing, they tells me, about losing money on her.

After the war, I comes to Raleigh and works for Major Russ, then I cooks a year on Hillsboro Street for somebody who I can't remember right now, then I goes to Louisburg to cook in Mr. Dedman's hotel, and hearing about Melissa, I finds that she am my sister, so I goes to Miz Mitchel's and I gets her.

A few years after the war, I marries Alex Dunson, who was a body slave for Major Fernie Green and went through all the war. Me and him lived together sixty years, I reckon, and he died the night before Thanksgiving in 1923.

Slavery wasn't so good, cause it divided families and done a heap of other things that was bad, but the work was good for everybody. It's a pity that these younguns nowadays don't know the value of work like we did. Why, when I was ten years old, I could do any kind of housework and spin and weave to boot. I hope that these chilluns will learn something in school and church. That's the only way they can learn it.

◆ ◆ ◆

Mattie Curtis

Age 98 when interviewed at
Route #4, Raleigh, N.C.,
by Mary A. Hicks

I WAS BORN ON the plantation of Mr. John Hayes
in Orange County ninety-eight years ago. Several of the chilluns had been sold before the speculator come and buyed Mammy, Pappy and we three
chilluns. The speculator was named Bebus, and he
lived in Henderson, but he meant to sell us in the
tobacco country.

We come through Raleigh, and the first thing
that I remembers good was going through the paper
mill on Crabtree. We traveled on to Granville County
on the Granville Tobacco Path till a preacher named
Whitfield buyed us. We lived near the Granville
and Franklin County line, on the Granville side.

Preacher Whitfield, being a preacher, was sup-
posed to be good, but he ain't half fed nor clothed
his slaves, and he whipped them bad. I seen him
whip my mammy with all the clothes off her back.
He'd buck her down on a barrel and beat the blood
out of her. There was some difference in his beating
from the neighbors. The folks round there would
whip in the back yard, but Marse Whitfield would
have the barrel carried in his parlor for the beating.

Speaking about clothes, I went as naked as your
hand till I was fourteen years old. I was naked like

that when my nature come to me. Marse Whitfield ain't caring, but after that, Mammy told him that I had to have clothes.

We ain't had no sociables, but we went to church on Sunday, and they preached to us that we'd go to hell alive if we sassed our white folks.

Marse Whitfield ain't never pay for us, so finally we was sold to Miz Fanny Long in Franklin County. That woman was a devil if there ever was one. When I was little, I had picked up the fruit, fanned flies off the table with a peafowl fan and nursed the little slave chilluns. The last two or three years I had worked in the field, but at Miz Long's I worked in the tobacco factory. Yes ma'am, she had a tobacco factory where tobacco was stemmed, rolled, and packed in cases for selling. They said that she had got rich on selling chewing tobacco.

We was at Miz Long's when war was declared. Before that she had been pretty good, but she was a devil now. Her son was called to the war, and he won't go. They come and arrest him; then his mammy try to pay him out, but that ain't no good. The officers says that he was yeller, and that they was going to shoot his head off and use it for a soap gourd. The Yankees did shoot him down here at Bentonville, and Miz Long went after the body. The Confederates has got the body but they won't let her have it for love nor money. They laugh and tell her how yeller he was, and they buried him in a ditch like a dog.

I don't know how come it, but just before the end of the war, we come to Moses Mordicia's place, right up the hill from here. He was mean too, he'd get drunk and whip niggers all day, off and on. He'd keep them tied down that long too, sometimes from sunrise till dark.

Mr. Mordicia had his yeller gals in one quarter to theirselves, and these gals belong to the Mordicia men, their friends, and the overseers. When a baby was born in that quarter, they'd send it over to the black quarter at birth. They do say that some of these gal babies got grown, and after going back to the yeller quarter, had more chilluns for her own daddy or brother. The Thompsons sprung from that set, and they say that a heap of them is halfwits for the reason that I just told you. Them yeller women was highfalutin', too; they thought they was better than the black ones. Have you ever wondered why the yeller women these days are meaner than black ones about the men? Well, that's the reason for it, their mammies raised them to think about the white men.

When the Yankees come, they come and freed us. The woods was full of Rebs what had deserted, but the Yankees killed some of them.

Right after the war, northern preachers come around with a little book a-marrying slaves, and I seed one of them marry my pappy and mammy. After this, they tried to find their fourteen oldest chilluns what was sold away, but they never did find but three of them.

Some sort of corporation cut the land up, but the slaves ain't got none of it that I ever heard about. I got married before the war to Joshua Curtis. Josh ain't really care about no home, but through this land corporation I buyed these fifteen acres on time. I cut down the big trees that was all over these fields, and I mauled out the wood and sold it, then I plowed up the fields and planted them. Josh did help to build the house, and he worked out some.

I done a heap of work at night too, all of my sewing and such, and the piece of land near the house over there ain't never got no work except at night. I finally paid for the land. Some of my chilluns was born in the field, too. When I was to the house, we had a granny, and I blowed in a bottle to make the labor quick and easy. All of this time I had nineteen chilluns, and Josh died, but I kept on, and the fifteen what is dead lived to be near about grown, every one of them.

I'll never forget my first bale of cotton and how I got it sold. I was some proud of that bale of cotton, and after I had it ginned, I set out with it on my steer cart for Raleigh. The white folks hated the nigger then, specially the nigger what was making something, so I dasn't ask nobody where the market was. I thought that I could find the place by myself, but I rid all day and had to take my cotton home with me that night, 'cause I can't find no place to sell it at. But that night I think it over, and the next day I go back and ask a policeman about the market. Lo and behold, child, I found it on Blount Street, and I had pass by it several times the day before.

This young generation ain't worth shucks. Fifteen years ago I hired a big buck nigger to help me shrub, and before eleven o'clock he passes out on me. You know about eleven o'clock in July it gets in a bloom. The young generation with their schools and their divorcing ain't going to get nothing out of life. It was better when folks just lived together. Their loafing gets them into trouble, and their novels makes them bad husbands and wives too.

♦ ♦ ♦

Jacob Manson

Age 86 when interviewed at
317 N. Haywood Street, Raleigh, N.C.,
by T. Pat Matthews

I BELONGED TO COLONEL Bun Eden. His plantation was in Warren County, and he owned about fifty slaves or more. There was so many of them there he did not know all his own slaves.

Our cabins was built of poles and had stick-and-dirt chimneys, one door, and one little window at the back end of the cabin. Some of the houses had dirt floors. Our clothing was poor and homemade.

Many of the slaves went bareheaded and barefooted. Some wore rags around their heads, and some wore bonnets. We had poor food, and the young slaves was fed out of troughs. The food was put in a trough, and the little niggers gathered around and et. The chillun was looked after by the old slave women who were unable to work in the fields, while the mothers of the babies worked. The women plowed and done other work as the men did. No books or learning of any kind was allowed. No prayer meetings was allowed, but we sometimes went to the white folks' church. They told us to obey our marsters and be obedient at all times.

When bad storms come, they let us rest, but they kept us in the fields so long sometimes that the storm caught us before we could get to the cabins.

Niggers watched the weather in slavery time, and the old ones was good at prophesying the weather.

Marster lived in the great house. He did not do any work but drank a lot of whiskey, went dressed up all the time, and had niggers to wash his feet and comb his hair. He made me scratch his head when he lay down, so he could go to sleep. When he got to sleep, I would slip out. If he waked up when I started to leave, I would have to go back and scratch his head till he went to sleep again. Sometimes I had to fan the flies away from him while he slept.

Marster would not have any white overseers. He had nigger foremen. Ha! Ha! He liked some of the nigger womens too good to have any other white man playing around them. He had his sweethearts among his slave women. I ain't no man for telling false stories. I tells the truth, and that is the truth. At that time, it was a hard job to find a marster that didn't have women among his slaves. That was a general thing among the slave owners. One of the slave girls on a plantation near us went to her missus and told her about her marster forcing her to let him have something to do with her, and her missus told her, "Well, go on, you belong to him."

A lot of the slave owners had certain strong, healthy slave men to serve the slave women. Generally they give one man four women, and that man better not have nothing to do with the other women, and the women better not have nothing to do with other men.

We worked all day and some of the night, and a slave who made a week, even after doing that, was lucky if he got off without getting a beating. We got mighty bad treatment, and I just want to tell you, a nigger didn't stand as much show there as a dog did. They whipped for most any little trifle. They whipped me, so they said, just to help me get a quicker gait.

The pattyrollers come sneaking around often and whipped niggers on Marster's place. They nearly killed my uncle. They broke his collarbone when they was beating him, and Marster made them pay for it 'cause Uncle never did get over it.

One morning the dogs begun to bark, and in a few minutes the plantation was covered with Yankees. They told us we was free. They asked me where Marster's things was hid. I told them I could not give up Marster's things. They told me I had no marster, that they had fighted four years to free us and that Marster would not whip me no more. Marster sent to the fields and had all the slaves to come home. He told me to tell them not to run but to fly to the house at once. All plowhands and women come running home. The Yankees told all of them they was free.

Marster offered some of the Yankees something to eat in his house, but they would not eat cooked food, they said they wanted to cook their own food.

After the war, I farmed around, one plantation to another. I have never owned a home of my own. When I got too old to work, I come and lived with my married daughter in Raleigh. I been here four years.

I think slavery was a mighty bad thing, though it's been no bed of roses since, but then no one could whip me no more.

◆ ◆ ◆

Mary Anderson

*Age 86 when interviewed August 23, 1937
at 17 Poole Road, R.F.D. #2, Raleigh, N.C.,
by T. Pat Matthews*

I WAS BORN ON a plantation near Franklinton, Wake County, North Carolina, May 10, 1851. I was a slave belonging to Sam Brodie, who owned the plantation. My missus' name was Evaline. My father was Alfred Brodie, and my mother was Bertha Brodie.

The plantation was very large, and there were about two hundred acres of cleared land that was farmed each year. We had good food, plenty of warm, homemade clothes, and comfortable houses. The slave houses were called the quarters, and the house where Marster lived was called the great house. Our houses had two rooms each, and Marster's house had twelve rooms. Both the slave and the white folks' buildings were located in a large grove one mile square covered with oak and hickory nut trees. Marster's house was exactly one mile from the main Louisburg Road, and there was a wide avenue leading through the plantation and grove to Marster's house. The house fronted the avenue east, and in going down the avenue from the main road you traveled directly west.

Many of the things we used were made on the

place. There was a grist mill, tannery, shoe shop, blacksmith shop, and looms for weaving cloth.

Marster had a large apple orchard in the Tar River low grounds, and up on higher ground and nearer the plantation house there was on one side of the road a large plum orchard, and on the other side was an orchard of peaches, cherries, quinces, and grapes. We picked the quinces in August and used them for preserving. Marster and Missus believed in giving the slaves plenty of fruit, especially the children.

A pond was located on the place, and in winter ice was gathered there for summer use and stored in an icehouse, which was built in the grove where the other buildings were. A large hole about ten feet deep was dug in the ground; the ice was put in that hole and covered. A large frame building was built over it. At the top of the earth, there was an entrance door and steps leading down to the bottom of the hole. Other things besides ice were stored there. There was a still on the plantation, and barrels of brandy were stored in the icehouse—also pickles, preserves, and cider.

There were about 162 slaves on the plantation, and every Sunday morning, all the children had to be bathed, dressed, and their hair combed, and carried down to Marster's for breakfast. It was a rule that all the little colored children eat at the great house every Sunday morning in order that Marster and Missus could watch them eat, so they could know which ones were sickly and have them doctored.

The slave children all carried a mussel shell in their hands to eat with. The food was put on large trays and the children all gathered around and ate, dipping up their food with their mussel shells, which they used for spoons. Those who refused to eat or those who were ailing in any way had to come back to the great house for their meals and medicine until they were well. Sunday was a great day on the plantation. Everybody got biscuits Sundays. The slave women went down to Marster's for their Sunday allowance of flour.

Marster had three children, one boy named Dallas, and two girls, Lettie and Carrie. He would not allow slave children to call his children "Marster" and "Missus" unless the slave said "Little Marster" or "Little Missus." Marster's children and the slave children played together. I went around with the baby girl, Carrie, to other plantations visiting. She taught me how to talk low and how to act in company. My association with white folks and my training while I was a slave is why I talk like white folks.

We were allowed to have prayer meetings in our homes, and we also went to the white folks' church. They would not teach any of us to read and write. Books and papers were forbidden.

Pattyrollers were not allowed on the place unless they came peacefully, and I never knew of them whipping any slaves on Marster's place. He had four white overseers, but they were not allowed to whip a slave. If there was any whipping to be done, he always said he would do it. He didn't believe in whipping, so when a slave got so bad he could not manage him, he sold him. Slaves were carried off on two-horse wagons to be sold. I have seen several loads leave. They were the unruly ones. Sometimes he would bring back slaves; once he brought back two boys and three girls from the slave market.

The war was begun, and there were stories of fights and freedom. The news went from plantation to plantation, and while the slaves acted natural and some even more polite than usual, they prayed for freedom.

Then one day I heard something that sounded like thunder, and Missus and Marster began to walk around and act queer. The grown slaves were whispering to each other. Sometimes they gathered in little gangs in the grove. Next day I heard it again, boom, boom, boom. I went and asked Missus, "Is it going to rain?" She said, "Mary, go to the icehouse and bring me some pickles and preserves." I went and got them. She ate a little and gave me some. Then she said, "You run along and play." In a day or two, everybody on the plantation seemed to be disturbed, and Marster and Missus were crying. Marster ordered all the slaves to come to the great house at nine o'clock. Nobody was working, and slaves were walking over the grove in every direction.

At nine o'clock, all the slaves gathered at the great house, and Marster and Missus come out on the porch and stood side by side. You could hear a pin drop, everything was so quiet. Then Marster said, "Good morning," and Missus said, "Good morning, children." They were both crying. Then Marster said, "Men, women, and children, you are free. You are no longer my slaves. The Yankees will soon be here."

Marster and Missus then went into the house, got two large armchairs, put them on the porch facing the avenue, and sat down side by side and remained there watching. In about an hour, there was one of the blackest clouds coming up the avenue from the main road. It was the Yankee soldiers. They finally filled the milelong avenue reaching from Marster's house to the main Louisburg Road and spread out over the mile-square grove.

The mounted men dismounted. The footmen stacked their shining guns and began to build fires and cook. They called the slaves, saying, "You are free." Slaves were whooping and laughing and acting like they were crazy. Yankee soldiers were shaking hands with the Negroes and calling them Sam, Dinah, Sarah, and asking them questions. They busted the door to the smokehouse and got all the hams. They went to the icehouse and got several barrels of brandy, and such a time. The Negroes and Yankees were cooking and eating together. The Yankees told them to come on and join them, they were free.

Marster and Missus sat on the porch, and they were so humble no Yankee bothered anything in the great house. The slaves were awfully excited. The Yankees stayed there, cooked, eat, drank, and played music until about night. Then a bugle began to blow and you never saw such getting on horses and lining up in your life. In a few minutes they began to march, leaving the grove, which was soon as silent as a graveyard. They took Marster's horses and cattle with them and joined the main army and camped just across Cypress Creek one and one-half miles from my Marster's place on the Louisburg Road.

When they left the country, lot of the slaves went with them, and soon there were none of Marster's slaves left. They wandered around for a year from place to place, fed and working most of the time at some other slave owner's plantation and getting more homesick every day.

The second year after the surrender, our marster and missus got on their carriage and went and looked up all the Negroes they heard of who ever belonged to them. Some who went off with the Yankees were never heard of again. When Marster and Missus found any of theirs, they would say, "Well, come back home."

My father and mother, two uncles, and their families moved back. Also Lorenza Brodie, and John Brodie, and their families moved back. Several of the young men and women who once belonged to him came back. Some were so glad to get back they cried, 'cause fare had been mighty bad part of the time they were rambling around, and they were hungry. When they got back, Marster would say, "Well, you have come back home, have you?" and the Negroes would say, "Yes, Marster." Most all spoke of them as Miss and Marster as they did before the surrender, and getting back home was the greatest pleasure of all.

We stayed with Marster and Missus and went to their church, the Maple Springs Baptist Church, until they died.

Bettie Brodie married a Dr. Webb from Boylan, Virginia. Carrie married a Mr. Joe Green of Franklin County. He was a big Southern planter.

Since the Surrender, I married James Anderson. I had four children, one boy and three girls.

I think slavery was a mighty good thing for Mother, Father, me, and the other members of the family, and I cannot say anything but good for my old marster and missus, but I can only speak for those whose conditions I have known during slavery and since. For myself and them, I will say again, slavery was a mighty good thing.

Thomas Hall

Age 81 when interviewed
September 10, 1937
at 316 Tarboro road, Raleigh, N.C.,
by T. Pat Matthews

MY NAME IS THOMAS Hall and I was born in Orange County, North Carolina, on a plantation belonging to Jim Woods, whose wife, our missus, was named Folly. I am eighty-one years of age, as I was born February 14, 1856. My father, Daniel Hall, and my mother Becke Hall and me all belonged to the same man, but it was often the case that this was not true, as one man, perhaps a Johnson, would own a husband and a Smith own the wife, each slave going by the name of the slave owner's family. In such cases, the children went by the name of the family to which the mother belonged.

Getting married and having a family was a joke in the days of slavery, as the main thing in allowing any form of matrimony among the slaves was to raise more slaves in the same sense and for the same purpose as stock raisers raise horses and mules, that is, for work. A woman who could produce fast was in great demand and would bring a good price on the auction block in Richmond, Virginia; Charleston, South Carolina; and other places.

The food in many cases that was given the slaves was not given them for their pleasure or by a cheerful giver, but for the simple and practical reason that children would not grow into a large healthy slave unless they were well fed and clothed, and given good warm places in which to live.

Conditions and rules were bad and the punishments were severe and barbarous. Some marsters acted like savages. In some instances slaves were burned at the stake. Families were torn apart by selling. Mothers were sold from their children. Children were sold from their mothers, and the father was not considered in any way as a family part. These conditions were here before the Civil War, and the conditions in a changed sense have been here ever since. The whites have always held the slaves in part slavery and are still practicing the same things on them in a different manner. Whites lynch, burn, and persecute the Negro race in America yet, and there is little they are doing to help them in any way.

Lincoln got the praise for freeing us, but did he do it? He give us freedom without giving us any chance to live to ourselves, and we still had to depend on the Southern white man for work, food, and clothing, and he held us, through our necessity and want, in a state of servitude but little better than slavery. Lincoln done but little for the Negro race, and from living standpoint, nothing. White folks are not going to do nothing for Negroes except keep them down.

Harriet Beecher Stowe, the writer of *Uncle Tom's Cabin,* did that for her own good. She had her own interests at heart, and I don't like her, Lincoln, or none of the crowd. The Yankees helped free us, so they say, but they let us be put back in slavery again.

When I think of slavery, it makes me mad. I do not believe in giving you my story, because with all the promises that have been made, the Negro is still in a bad way in the United States, no matter in what part he lives, it's all the same. Now you may be all right; there are a few white men who are, but the pressure is such from your white friends that you will be compelled to talk against us and give us the cold shoulder when you are around them, even if your heart is right towards us.

You are going around to get a story of slavery conditions and the persecutions of Negroes before the Civil War and the economic conditions concerning them since that war. You should have known before this late date all about that. Are you going to help us? No! You are only helping yourself. You say that my story may be put into a book, that you are from the Federal Writers' Project. Well, the Negro will not get anything out of it, no matter where you are from. Harriet Beecher Stowe wrote *Uncle Tom's Cabin*. I didn't like her book, and I hate her. No matter where you are from, I don't want you to write my story, because the white folks have been and are now and always will be against the Negro.

Sarah Debro

*Age 90 when interviewed
July 24, 1937 at Durham, N.C.,
by Travis Jordan*

I WAS BORN IN Orange County way back some time in the fifties. Miz Polly White Cain and Marse Dr. Cain was my white folks. Marse Cain's plantation joined Mr. Paul Cameron's land. Marse Cain owned so many niggers that he didn't know his own slaves when he met them in the road. Sometimes he would stop them and say: "Whose niggers are you?" They'd say, "We's Marse Cain's niggers." Then he would say, "I's Marse Cain," and drive on.

Marse Cain was good to his niggers. He didn't whip them like some owners did, but if they done mean, he sold them. They knew this so they minded him. One day Grandpappy sassed Miss Polly White, and she told him that if he didn't behave hisself that she would put him in her pocket. Grandpappy was a big man, and I ask him how Miss Polly could do that. He said she meant that she would sell him, then put the money in her pocket. He never did sass Miss Polly no more.

I was kept at the big house to wait on Miss Polly, to tote her basket of keys and such as that. Whenever she seed a child down in the quarters that she wanted to raise by hand, she took them up to the big house and trained them. I was to be a house-

46

maid. The day she took me, my mammy cried, 'cause she knew I would never be allowed to live at the cabin with her no more. Miss Polly was big and fat and she made us niggers mind, and we had to keep clean. My dresses and aprons was starched stiff. I had a clean apron every day. We had white sheets on the beds, and we niggers had plenty to eat too, even ham. When Miss Polly went to ride, she took me in the carriage with her. The driver set way up high, and me and Miss Polly set way down low. They was two hosses with shiny harness. I toted Miss Polly's bag and bundles, and if she dropped her handkerchief, I picked it up. I loved Miss Polly and loved staying at the big house.

I was about waist high when the soldiers mustered. I went with Miss Polly down to the mustering field where they was marching. I can see they feets now, when they flung them up and down, saying hep, hep. When they was all ready to go and fight, the women folks fixed a big dinner. Aunt Charity and Pete cooked two or three days for Miss Polly. The table was piled with chicken, ham, shoat, barbecue, young lamb, and all sorts of pies, cakes, and things, but nobody eat nothing much. Miss Polly and the ladies got to crying. The vittles got cold. I was so sad that I got over in the corner and cried too. The men folks all had on they new soldier clothes, and they didn't eat nothing neither. Young Marse Jim went up and put his arm around Miss Polly, his mammy, but that made her cry harder. Marse Jim was a cavalry. He rode a big hoss, and my Uncle Dave went with him to the field as his bodyguard. He had a hoss too, so if Marse Jim's hoss got shot, there would be another one for him to ride. Miss Polly had another son, but he was too drunk to hold a gun. He stayed drunk.

The first cannon I heard scared me near about to death. We could hear them going boom, boom. I thought it was thunder, then Miss Polly say, "Listen, Sarah, hear them cannons? They's killing our mens." Then she begun to cry.

I run in the kitchen where Aunt Charity was cooking and told her Miss Polly was crying. She said, "She ain't crying 'cause the Yankees killing the mens; she's doing all that crying 'cause she scared we's going to be set free." Then I got mad and told her Miss Polly wasn't like that.

I remember when Wheeler's Cavalry come through. They was 'federates, but they was mean as the Yankees. They stole everything they could find and killed a pile of niggers. They come around checking. They ask the niggers if they wanted to be free. If they say yes, then they shot them down, but if they say no, they let them alone. They took three of my uncles out in the woods and shot they faces off.

I remember the first time the Yankees come. They come galloping down the road, jumping over the palings, trompling down the rose bushes and messing up the flower beds. They stomped all over the house, in the kitchen, pantries, smokehouse, and everywhere, but they didn't find much, 'cause near about everything done been hid. I was setting on the steps when a big Yankee come up. He had on a cap, and his eyes was mean.

"Where did they hide the gold and silver, nigger?" he yelled at me.

I was scared, and my hands was ashy, but I told him I didn't know nothing about nothing; that if anybody done hid things, they hid it while I was asleep.

"Go ask that old white-headed devil," he said to me.

I got mad then, 'cause he was talking about Miss Polly, so I didn't say nothing, I just set. Then he pushed me off the step and say if I didn't dance, he going shoot my toes off. Scared as I was, I sure done some shuffling. Then he give me five dollars and told me to go buy jimcracks, but that piece of paper won't no good. 'Twasn't nothing but a shinplaster, like all that war money, you couldn't spend it.

That Yankee kept calling Miss Polly a whiteheaded devil and said she done ramshacked till they wasn't nothing left, but he made his mens tote off meat, flour, pigs, and chickens. After that, Miss Polly got mighty stingy with the vittles and we didn't have no more ham.

When the war was over, the Yankees was all around the place, telling the niggers what to do. They told them they was free, that they didn't have to slave for the white folks no more. My folks all left Marse Cain and went to live in houses that the Yankees built. They was like poor white folks' houses, little shacks made out of sticks and mud, with stick-and-mud chimneys. They wasn't like Marse Cain's cabins, planked up and warm, they was full of cracks, and they wasn't no lamps and oil. All the light come from the lightwood knots burning in the fireplace.

One day my mammy come to the big house after me. I didn't want to go, I wanted to stay with Miss Polly. I begun to cry, and Mammy caught hold of me. I grabbed Miss Polly and held so tight that I tore her skirt binding loose, and her skirt fell down about her feets.

"Let her stay with me," Miss Polly said to Mammy.

But Mammy shook her head. "You took her away from me and didn't pay no mind to my crying, so now I's taking her back home. We's free now, Miss Polly, we ain't going to be slaves no more to nobody." She dragged me away. I can see how Miss Polly looked now. She didn't say nothing, but she looked hard at Mammy, and her face was white.

Mammy took me to the stick-and-mud house the Yankees done give her. It was smoky and dark cause they wasn't no windows. We didn't have no sheets and no towels, so when I cried and said I didn't want to live in no Yankee house, Mammy beat me and made me go to bed. I laid on the straw tick looking up through the cracks in the roof. I could see the stars, and the sky shining through the cracks looked like long blue splinters stretched across the rafters. I lay there and cried 'cause I wanted to go back to Miss Polly.

I was never hungry till we was free and the Yankees fed us. We didn't have nothing to eat except hardtack and middling meat. You could boil it all day and all night and it wouldn't cook done. I wouldn't eat it. I thought 'twas mule meat; mules that done been shot on the battlefield then dried. I still believe 'twas mule meat.

One day me and my brother was looking for acorns in the woods. We found something like a grave in the woods. I told Dave they was something buried in that mound. We got the grubbing hoe and dug. They was a box with eleven hams in that grave. Somebody done hid it from the Yankees and forgot where they buried it. We covered it back up, 'cause if we took it home in the daytime, the Yankees and niggers would take it away from us. So when night come, we slipped out and toted them hams to the house and hid them in the loft.

Them was bad days. I'd rather been a slave than to been hired out like I was, 'cause I wasn't no field hand, I was a handmaid, trained to wait on the ladies. Then too, I was hungry most of the time and had to keep fighting off them Yankee mens. Them Yankees was mean folks.

We's come a long way since them times. I's lived near about ninety years, and I's seen and heard much. My folks don't want me to talk about slavery, they's shame niggers ever was slaves. But, while for most colored folks freedom is the best, they's still some niggers that ought to be slaves now. These niggers that's done clean forgot the Lord; those that's always cutting and fighting and going in white folks' houses at night, they ought to be slaves. They ought to have an old marse with a whip to make them come when he say come and go when he say go, till they learn to live right.

I looks back and thinks. I ain't never forgot them slavery days, and I ain't never forgot Miss Polly and my white starched aprons.

Ria Sorrell

Age 97 when interviewed
August 23, 1937
at 536 E. Edenton Street, Raleigh, N.C.,
by T. Pat Matthews

I JUST LACK THREE years of being one hundred years old. I belonged to Jacob Sorrell. His wife was named Elizabeth. My age was given to me by Mr. Bob Sorrell, the only one of Old Marster's chilluns that is living now. I was born on Marster's plantation near Leesville, in Wake County. That's been a long time ago. I can't get around now like I could when I was on the plantation.

Our houses was good houses, 'cause Marster seed to it they was fixed right. We had good beds and plenty of cover. The houses was called the nigger houses. They was about two hundred yards from the big house. Our houses had two rooms, and Marster's had seven rooms.

We didn't have any overseer, Marster said he didn't believe in them and he didn't want any. The oldest slaves on the place woke us up in the morning and acted as foreman. Marster hardly ever went to the field. He told Squire Holman and Sam Sorrell, two old slaves, what he wanted done, and they told us and we done it. I worked at the house as nurse and housegirl most of the time.

Mother and Father worked in the field. Mother was named Judy, and Father was named Sam. You sees, Father was a slave foreman. Marster bought Squire Holman from the Holmans and let him keep his name. That's why he was called that.

We worked from sunup till sunset with a rest spell at twelve o'clock of two hours. He give us holidays to rest in. That was Christmas, a week off then, then a day every month, and all Sundays. He said he was a Christian and he believed in giving us a chance. He give us patches and all they made on it. He give slaves days off to work their patches.

We had prayer meeting any time, and we went to the white folks' church. There was no whiskey on the place, no, no, honey, no whiskey. Now at cornshuckings, they had a big supper and all et all they wanted. I'll tell you Jake Sorrell was all right. We didn't have any dances no time. Some nights Marster would come to our cabins, call us all into one of them, and pray with us. He stood up in the floor and told us all to be good and pray.

There was about twenty-five slaves on the place, and Marster just wouldn't sell a slave. When he whupped one, he didn't whup much; he was a good man. He seemed to be sorry every time he had to whup any of the slaves. His wife was a pure devil, she just joyed whupping Negroes. She was tall and spare-made with black hair and eyes. Over both her eyes was a bulge place in her forehead. Her eyes set way back in her head. Her jaws were large like a man's, and her chin stuck up. Her mouth was large, and her lips thin and seemed to be closed like she had something in her mouth most all the time.

When Marster come to town, she raised old scratch with the slaves. She whupped all she could while Marster was gone. She tried to boss Marster, but he wouldn't allow that. He kept her from whupping many a slave. She just wouldn't feed a slave, and when she had her way, our food was bad. She said underleaves of collards was good enough for slaves. Marster took feeding in his hands and fed us plenty at times. He said people couldn't work without eating. Many was the meals he give us unbeknown to his wife. Sometimes he brought hog haslets and good things to the nigger house and told us to cook it. When it was done, he come and et all he wanted, got up and said, "I'm going now," and you didn't see him no more till next day.

There was one thing they wouldn't allow, that was books and papers. I can't read and write.

I heard talk of Abraham Lincoln coming through when talk of the war come about. They met, him and Jeff Davis, in South Carolina. Lincoln said, "Jeff Davis, let them niggers go free." Jeff Davis told him, "You can't make us give up our property." Then the war started.

Yes, I remembers the Yankees. The Southern, our folks, was in front. They come along a road right by our house. Our folks was going on and the Yankees right behind. You could hear them shooting. They called it skirmishing. It was raining, and our folks was going through the mud and slush. They had wagons and some would say, "Drive up, God damn it, drive up, the damn Yankees right behind us." They had turkeys and chickens on the wagons and on their horses. They got things out of the houses and took the stock. They searched the houses and took the quilts and sheets and things.

The Yankees was soon there, and they done the same thing. That was a time. They took all they could find, and there wasn't much left when all got through. The Yankees poured out molasses and stomped down things they could not carry off. I was afraid of the Yankees. They come up and said,

"Hain't you got some money round here?" I told them I knowed nothing about money. They called me "auntie" and said, "Auntie, tell us where the money is, you knows." I says, "They don't let me see everything around here, no, that they don't."

When they told us we was free, we stayed right on with Marster. We got crackers and meat from the Yankees, and when the crop was housed in the fall, Marster gave us part of all we made. We come to Raleigh on a old steer cart to get our crackers and meat—that was our allowance. We stayed at Marster's till Father died. I married there.

Marster died of consumption. I saw him die. I saw him when the breath went out of him. The last word he said was, "Lord, do your will, not mine." Then he breathed twice and was no more. I sure believes Marster went to Heaven, but Missus, well, I don't know. Don't know about her, she was so bad. She would hide her baby's cap and tell me to find it. If I couldn't find it, she whupped me. She would call Marster, and I doing the best I could to please her, and say, "Come here, Jacob, and whup this nigger," but Marster paid no attention to her. He took our part.

We finally moved to the Page place, about eleven miles north of Raleigh. We been farming with the white folks ever since, till we got so we couldn't work.

I married Buck Sorrell since the surrender. We had four boys and two girls, six children in all. They are all dead, except one, her name is Bettie. She works at Dr. Rogers's.

Missus died since the surrender. When she got sick she sent for me to go and wait on her. I just couldn't refuse Missus when she sent for me, even if she had treated me bad. I went and cleaned her like a baby, waited on her till the evening she died, that night. I went off that evening late to spend the night, and next morning when I got there, she was dead.

A lot of the niggers in slavery time worked so hard, they said they hated to see the sun rise in the morning. Slavery was a bad thing, 'cause some white folks didn't treat their niggers right.

◆ ◆ ◆

Betty Cofer

*Age 81 when interviewed at
the Beverly Jones homestead in Wachovia,
by Esther S. Pinnix*

I CAN'T GET AROUND much, because my feet and legs bother me, but I got good eyes and good ears and all my own teeth. I ain't never had a bad tooth in my head. Yes'm, I'm eighty-one, going on eighty-two. Marster done wrote my age down in his book where he kept the names of all his colored folks. Ma belonged to Dr. Jones, but Pappy belonged to Marse Israel Lash over yonder. Younguns always went with their mammies, so I belonged to the Joneses. Ma and Pappy could visit back and forth sometimes, but they never lived together until after freedom.

Marster and old Miss Julia was mighty strict, but they was good to us. Colored folks on some of the other plantations wasn't so lucky. Some of them had overseers, mean, cruel men. On one plantation the field hands had to hustle to get to the end of the row at eleven o'clock dinnertime, because when the cooks brought their dinner, they had to stop just where they was and eat, and the sun was mighty hot out in those fields. They only had ashcakes, without salt, and molasses for their dinner, but we had beans and grits and salt and sometimes meat.

I was lucky. Miss Ella was a little girl when I was

borned, and she claimed me. We played together and grew up together. I waited on her and most times slept on the floor in her room. Ma was cook, and when I done got big enough, I helped to set the table in the big dining room. Then I'd put on a clean white apron and carry in the victuals and stand behind Miss Ella's chair. She'd fix me a piece of something from her plate and hand it back over her shoulder to me. I'd take it and run outside to eat it. Then I'd wipe my mouth and go back to stand behind Miss Ella again and maybe get another snack.

Yes'm, there was a crowd of hands on the plantation. I mind them all, and I can call most of their names. There was always two washwomen, a cook, some hands to help her, two sewing women, a housegirl, and some who did all the weaving and spinning. The men worked in the fields and yard. One was stable boss and looked after all the horses and mules. We raised our own flax and cotton and wool, spun the thread, wove the cloth, made all the clothes. Yes'm, we made the men's shirts and pants and coats. One woman knitted all the stockings for the white folks and colored folks too. I mind she had one finger all twisted and stiff from holding her knitting needles. We wove the cotton and linen for sheets and pillow slips and table covers. We wove the wool blankets too. I use to wait on the girl who did the weaving. When she took the cloth off the loom, she done give me the "thrums." I tied them all together with teensy little knots and got me some scraps from the sewing room, and I made me some quilt tops. Some of them was real pretty, too!

All our spinning wheels and flax wheels and looms was handmade by a wheelwright, Marse Noah Westmoreland. He lived over yonder. Those old wheels are still in the family. I got one of the flax wheels. Miss Ella done give it to me for a present. Leather was tanned and shoes was made on the place. Course, the hands mostly went barefoot in warm weather, white chillun too. We had our own mill to grind the wheat and corn, and we raised all our meat. We made our own candles from tallow and beeswax. I 'spect some of the old candle molds are over to the house now. We wove our own candlewicks too. I never saw a match till I was a grown woman. We made our fire with flint and punk. Yes'm, I was trained to cook and clean and sew. I learned to make men's pants and coats. First coat I made, Miss Julia told me to rip the collar off, and by the time I picked out all the teensy stitches and sewed it together again, I could set a collar right!

Miss Julia cut out all the clothes herself for men and women too. I 'spect her big shears and patterns and old cutting table are over at the house now. Miss Julia cut out all the clothes, and then the colored girls sewed them up, but she looked them all over, and they better be sewed right!

Miss Julia bossed the whole plantation. She looked after the sick folks and sent the doctor to dose them, and she carried the keys to the storerooms and pantries.

Yes'm, I'm some educated. Ma showed me my "a-b-abs" and my numbers, and when I was fifteen, I went to school in the log church built by the Moravians. They give it to the colored folks to use for their own school and church. Our teacher was a white man, Marse Fulk. He had one eye, done lost the other in the war. We didn't have no colored teachers then. They wasn't educated. We attended school four months a year. I went through the fifth reader, the *North Carolina Reader*. I can figger a little and read some, but I can't write much, 'cause my fingers are all stiffened up. Miss Julia use to read the Bible to us and tell us right and wrong, and Ma showed me all she could and so did the other colored folks.

No'm, I don't know much about spells and charms. Course most of the old folks believed in them. One colored man use to make charms, little bags filled with queer things. He called them jacks, and sold them to the colored folks and some white folks too.

Yes'm, I saw some slaves sold away from the plantation, four men and two women, both of them with little babies. The traders got them. Sold them down to Mobile, Alabama. One was my pappy's sister. We never heard from her again. I saw a likely young feller sold for fifteen hundred dollars. That was my Uncle Ike. Marse Jonathan Spease bought him and kept him the rest of his life.

Yes'm, we saw Yankee soldiers. They come marching by and stopped at the house. I wasn't scared, 'cause they was all talking and laughing and friendly, but they sure was hungry. They dumped the wet clothes out of the big washpot in the yard and filled it with water. Then they broke into the smokehouse and got a lot of hams and boiled them in the pot and ate them right there in the yard. The women cooked up a lot of corn pone for them and coffee too. Marster had a barrel of liquor put by, and the Yankees knocked the head in and filled their canteens. There wasn't ary drop left.

When we heard the soldiers coming, our boys turned the horses loose in the woods. The Yankees said they had to have them and would burn the house down if we didn't get them. So our boys whistled up the horses and the soldiers carried them all off. They carried off old Jenny-mule too, but let little Jack-mule go. When the soldiers was gone, the stable boss said, "If old Jenny-mule once gets loose, nobody on earth can catch her unless she wants. She'll be back!" Sure enough, in a couple of days, she come home by herself, and we worked the farm just with her and little Jack.

Some of the colored folks followed the Yankees away. Five or six of our boys went. Two of them traveled as far as Yadkinville but come back. The rest of them kept going and we never heard tell of them again.

Yes'm, when we was freed, Pappy come to get Ma and me. We stayed around here. Where could we go? These was our folks, and I couldn't go far away from Miss Ella. We moved out near Rural Hall and Pappy farmed, but I worked at the homeplace a lot.

When I was about twenty-four, Marse R.J. Reynolds come from Virginia and set up a tobacco factory. He fetched some hands with him. One was a likely young feller, named Cofer, from Patrick County, Virginia. I liked him, and we got married and moved back here to my folks. We started to buy our little place and raise a family. I done had four chillun, but two's dead. I got grandchillun and great-grandchillun close by. This is home to us. When we talk about the old homeplace, we just say "the house" cause there's only one house to us. The rest of the family was all fine folks and good to me, but I loved Miss Ella better'n anyone or anything else in the world. She was the best friend I ever had. If I ever wanted for anything, I just asked her and she give it to me or got it for me somehow. Once, when Cofer was in his last sickness, his sister come from East Liverpool, Ohio, to see him. I went to Miss Ella to borrow a little money. She didn't have no change, but she just took a ten-dollar bill from her purse and says, "Here you are, Betty, use what you need and bring me what's left."

I always did what I could for her too and stood by her—but one time. That was when we was little girls going together to fetch the mail. It was hot and dusty, and we stopped to cool off and wade in the branch. We heard a horse trotting and looked up and there was Marster switching his riding whip and looking at us. "Git for home, you two, and I'll tend to you," he says, and we got! But this time I let Miss Ella go to the house alone and I sneaked around to Granny's cabin and hid. I was afraid I'd get whupped! Another time, Miss Ella went to town and told me to keep up her fire whilst she was away. I fell asleep in the hearth and the fire done burnt out so's when Miss Ella come home the room was cold. She was mad as hops. Said she never had hit me, but she sure felt like doing it then.

Yes'm, I been here a right smart while. I done lived to see three generations of my white folks come and go, and they're the finest folks on earth. There use to be a regular burying ground for the plantation hands. The colored chillun use to play there, but I always played with the white chillun. Three of the old log cabins is there yet. One of them was the boys' cabin. They've got walls a foot thick and are used for storerooms now. After freedom, we buried out around our little churches, but some of the old grounds are plowed under and turned into pasture, 'cause the colored folks didn't get no deeds to them. It won't be long before I go too, but I'm going lie near my old home and my folks.

Yes'm, I remember Marse Israel Lash, my Pappy's marster. He was a low, thick-set man, very jolly and friendly. He was real smart and good too, 'cause his colored folks all loved him. He worked in the bank, and when the Yankees come, 'stead of shutting the door against them like the others did, he bid them welcome. So the Yankees done took the bank but give it back to him for his very own, and he kept it, but there was lots of bad feeling 'cause he never give folks the money they put in the old bank.

Miss Ella died two years ago. I was sick in the hospital, but the doctor come to tell me. I couldn't go to her burying. I sure missed her. There wasn't ever no one like her. Miss Kate and young Miss Julia still live at the house with their brother, Marse Lucian, but it don't seem right with Miss Ella gone. Life seems different, somehow, though there's lots of my young white folks and my own kin living round, and they're real good to me. But Miss Ella's gone!

Patsy Mitchner

Age 84 when interviewed July 2, 1937
at 432 McKee Street, Raleigh, N.C.,
by T. Pat Matthews

MY MARSTER LIVED WHERE the bus station now
is on the corner of Martin and McDowell
streets, in that old house that stands near there
now. I was born and bred in Raleigh and have
never lived out of Wake County. I belonged to
Alex Gorman, a paper man. He printed the *Spirit
of the Age,* a newspaper. I reckon you can find it in
the museum. I reckons they keeps all way back
yonder things in there just to remember by. He had
a lot of printers, both black and white. The slaves
turned the wheels the most of the time, and the
white mens done the printing. There was a big place
dug out at each side of the machine. One man
pulled it to him, and the other pulled it to him.
They worked it with they hands. It was a big wheel.
They didn't have no printers then like they got now.

The old printing place is standing now. It stands
in front of the laundry on Dawson Street, where a
lot of red wagons stands going up towards the bus
station. The old building with stairsteps to go up.
They set the type upstairs, and the machine was on
the ground floor.

Marster married Gormans twice and they was
both named Mary. Don't know whether they was

sisters or not, but they was both Virginia women. So my missus' name was Mary Gorman.

I never seed my father in my life. My mother was named Tempe Gorman. They would not talk to me about who my father was nor where he was at. Mother would laugh sometime when I asked her about him.

Marster treated his niggers mean sometimes. He beat my mother till the scars was on her back, so I could see them.

They sold my mother, sister, and brother to old man Askew, a slave speculator, and they were shipped to the Mississippi bottoms in a boxcar. I never heard from mother any more. I never seed my brother again, but my sister come back to Charlotte. She come to see me. She married and lived there till she died.

In slavery time, the food was bad at Marster's. It was cooked one day for the next, that is, the corn bread was baked and the meat was boiled and you et it cold for breakfast. The meat was as fat as butter, and you got one ration and a hunk of corn bread for a meal. No biscuit was seen in the slave houses. No sir, that they was not. No biscuit for niggers at Marster's.

Our clothes was bad, and our sleeping places was just bunks. Our shoes had wooden bottoms on them.

I heard them talk about pattyrollers so much I was scared so I could hardly sleep at night sometimes. I was afraid they would come and catch me, but I never seed one in my life. I never seed any slaves sold, in chains, or a jail for slaves. I never seed a slave whupped. Marster took them in the back shed room to whup them.

We was not teached to read and write. You better not be caught with no paper in your hand; if you was, you got the cowhide. I dasn't to talk back to them; no matter what happened, they would get you if you talked back to them.

Old Dr. Jim McKee, who is dead and gone, looked after us when we was sick. He give us medicine and kept us clean out better than people is clean out now. Dr. John McKee at the City Hall is his son. They pays no attention to me now; guess they has forgotten me.

I do not know my age, but I was about twelve years old when Wheeler's Cavalry come through. They scared me so much I squatted like a rat. They pulled clothes off the line and stole clothes from stores and went down to the depot and changed clothes. They stole the women's drawers and filled them with things. They stole meat, corn, and other things and put them in women's drawers, throwed them across their horses' backs and went on. You know women then wore long drawers open in front. Ha! Ha! Wheeler's Cavalry tied up the legs and front of them and filled the legs and seat full of things they stole. They just grabbed everything and went on. They had a reason for leaving; the Yankees was at their heels.

Just as soon as they left, the Yankees come. You know, there was a man here by the name of Governor Holden, and the flag was a red and white flag, and when the Yankees come, there was another flag run up.

I want to try to tell the truth, 'cause I was teached that way by Marster and Missus.

The flag brought peace, because the Yankees did not tear up the town. They had guards out around the houses and they marched back and forth day and night to keep everybody from robbing the houses.

The Yankees with their blue uniforms on just covered the town. They was just like ants. They played pretty music on the band, and I liked that. I was afraid of them, though, 'cause Marster and Missus said they were going to give us to them when they come. I stayed hid most of the time right after the surrender, 'cause I didn't want the Yankees to catch me.

When the others left after the surrender, I run away and went to Rev. Louis Edwards, a nigger preacher. He sent me to my aunt at Rolesville. My aunt was named Patsy Lewis. I stayed there about three weeks, when my uncle rented where Cameron Park is now and tended it that year. We all come to Raleigh, and I have lived here all my life, but the three weeks I stayed at Rolesville.

Before two years had passed after the surrender, there was two out of every three slaves who wished they was back with their marsters. The marsters' kindness to the niggers after the war is the cause of the nigger having things today. There was a lot of love between marster and slave, and there is few of us that don't love the white folks today. I have worked for white folks, washing, cooking, and working at a laundry ever since freedom come.

I married Tom Mitchner after the war. I went by the name of Patsy Gorman till I was married. Now I goes by the name of Patsy Mitchner. My husband, Tom Mitchner, was born a slave.

The people is worser now than they was in slavery time. We need pattyrollers right now. 'Twould stop some of this stealing and keep a lot of folks out of the penitentiary. We need them right now.

Slavery was better for us than things is now, in some cases. Niggers then didn't have no responsibility, just work, obey, and eat. Now they got to shuffle around and live on just what the white folks mind to give them. Slaves prayed for freedom. Then they got it and didn't know what to do with it. They was turned out with nowhere to go and nothing to live on. They had no experience in looking out for themselves, and nothing to work with, and no land.

They make me think of the crowd one time who prayed for rain, when it was dry in crop time. The rain fell in torrents and kept falling till it was about a flood. The rain frogs begin to holler and calling more rain, and it rained and rained. Then the raincrow got up in a high tree, and he holler and asked the Lord for rain. It rained till every little rack of cloud that come over brought a big shower of large drops. The fields was so wet and miry you could not go in them, and water was standing in the fields middle of every row, while the ditches in the fields looked like little rivers, they was so full of water. It begun to thunder again in the southwest, right where we call the chubhole of the sky, where so much rain comes from, and the clouds growed blacker and blacker back there.

Then one of the mens who had been praying for rain up and said, "I tell you, brothers, if it don't quit raining, everything going to be washed away." They all looked at the black rain cloud in the west with sorrowful faces as if they felt they didn't know what use they had for rain after they got it. Then one of the brothers said to the other brothers, kinder easy and shameful like, "Brothers, don't you think we overdone this thing?"

That's what many a slave thought about praying for freedom.

Slavery was a bad thing, and freedom, of the kind we got, with nothing to live on, was bad. Two snakes full of poison. One lying with his head pointing north, the other with his head pointing south. Their names was slavery and freedom. The snake called slavery lay with his head pointed south, and the snake called freedom lay with his head pointed north. Both bit the nigger, and they was both bad.

Parker Pool

Age 91 when interviewed
by T. Pat Matthews

I WAS BORN NEAR Garner, Wake County, North Carolina. I belonged to Aufy Pool. He was a slave owner. His plantation was near Garner. I am ninety-one years old. I was born August 10, that's what my grandmammy told me, and I ain't never forgot it.

My missus' name was Betsy. My first master—I had two—was Master Aufy Pool. Then he give us to his son, or his son bought us in at the sale when Master Aufy died. After Master Aufy died, his son, Louis Pool, was my master then, and his plantation was in Johnston County. My mother was named Violet Pool. She died in childbirth two years after I was born. My father was named Peter Turner. He belonged to John Turner in Johnston County, right near Clayton.

My grandfather—I had two grandfathers, one on my mother's side and one on my father's side. On my mother's side, Tom Pool, on my father's side, Jerry Beddingfield. I never seed my great-grandparents, but my great-grandfather was named Buck. He was right out of Africa. His wife was name Hagar. I never have seen them, but my grandmother was their daughter. They had three chillun

70

here in America. My grandmammy and grandfather told me this. My brothers were name, oldest one, Haywood, then Lem, and Peter, and me, Parker Pool. The girls, oldest girl was Minerva Rilla.

I had good owners. My missus and master, they took just as good care of me as they could. They was good to all the hands. They give us plenty to eat, and we had plenty of clothes, such as they was, but there was no such clothes as we have now. They treated us good, I will have to say that. They are dead in their graves, but I will have to say this for them. Our houses were in the grove. We called Master's house the great house. We called our homes the houses. We had good places to sleep.

We got up at light. I had to do most of the nursing of the chillun, 'cause when chopping time come, the women had to go to work. We had plenty to eat, and we et it. Our something to eat was well fixed and cooked. We caught a lot of possums, coons, and other game, but I tell you, a coon is a lot harder to catch than a possum. We had one garden, and the colored people tended the garden, and we all et out'n it.

There was about two thousand acres in the plantation. All the farm land was fenced in with wood rails. The hogs, cows, and stock was turned out in the woods, and let go. The cows was drived home at night, that is, if they didn't come up. That is so we could milk the ones we wanted to milk.

We dug ditches to drain the land, blind ditches; we dug them and then put poles on top, and covered them with brush and dirt. We put the brush on the poles to keep the dirt from running through. Then we plowed over the ditches.

We tanned our leather in a tan trough. We used

white oak bark and red oak bark. They put copperas in it too, I think.

I knows how to raise flax. You grow it, and when it is grown, you pull it clean up out of the ground till it kinda rots. They have what they called a brake, then it was broke up in that. The bark was the flax. They had a stick called a swingle stick, made kinda like a sword. They used this to knock the sticks out of the flax. They would then put the flax on a hackle, a board with a lot of pegs in it. Then they clean and string it out till it looks like your hair. The flax when it came from the hackles was ready for the wheel, where it was spun into thread. I tell you, you couldn't break it, either.

When it was spun into thread, they put it on a reel. It turned 100 times and struck; when it struck, it was called a cut. When it come from the wheel, it was called a broach. The cuts stood for so much flax. So many cuts made a yard, but there was more to do—size it, and hank it—before it was weaved. Most of the white people had flax clothes.

We had no church on the plantation. We had prayer meeting and candy-pullings, and we would ask slaves from other plantations. My master had no public cornshuckings. His slaves shucked his corn. He had about fifty head. The slaves, they went to the white folks' church. They had a place separate from the white folks by a railing. We could look at the preacher and hear him preach too.

No, sirree, they wouldn't let us have no books. They would not let none of the chilluns tell us anything about a book. I can't read and write, not a bit. They preached to us to obey our master. Preacher John Ellington was my favorite preacher. No nigger was allowed to preach. They was allowed to pray and shout sometimes, but they better not be catched with a book. The songs that they sung then, they hardly ever sing them now. They were the good old songs. "Hark from the Tomb, the Doleful Sound."

I seed many pattyrollers during slavery. If they caught you out at night without a pass, they would whup you. We visited at night, during slavery time. The men went courting. When a man, a slave, loved a woman on another plantation, they asked their master, sometimes the master would ask the other master. If they agreed, all the slave man and woman had to do Saturday night was for him to come over and they would go to bed together. There was no marriage until after the surrender. All who wanted to keep the same woman after the surrender had to pay twenty-five cents for a marriage license, then a dollar and a half, then three dollars. If the magistrate married you, you didn't have to pay anything, unless he charged you.

We got the holidays, Christmas, and after lay-by time of the crops. They had big dinners then. They had big tables set in the yard, the rations was spread on them, and everybody et. We had brandy at Christmas.

We had good doctors when we got sick. I remembers Dr. James, of Clayton, coming to our house. They carried their pills and medicine then, and left it at the house for you.

I have been whupped twice, and I have seen slaves whupped. Ha! Ha! Missus whupped me. She wouldn't let nobody else whup me, neither. I remembers what it was about as if it was yesterday. She was fretted about the cook. We was skinning Irish taters. She told us to make haste; if we didn't make haste and peel the taters, she would whack us down. I laughed; she sent me to get a switch. She hit me on the legs. When we were whupped, we would say, "Oh! Pray," and they would quit. If you acted stubborn, they would whup you more.

She asked me, "Ain't you going to say, 'Oh! Pray?' "

I was mad. She was not hurting me much, and I wouldn't say nothing. After awhile, I said, "Oh! Pray," and she quit.

I had good owners, all of them. My masters never did hit me. Missus would not whup me much. She just wanted to show off sometimes.

My master had a son in the war, Walter Pool. He was a foot soldier at first. He got sick, and he come home sick on furlough. He hired a man to go in his place at first, then the man went. After awhile, the men got so scarce, he had to go again; then he got the chance to go in the cavalry. Old Master bought him a horse, and he could ride next time. He belonged to the First Georgia Regiment, Second Cavalry, General Dange's Brigade, C Company, North Carolina Volunteers.

I saw the Confederates' General Johnson come through Clayton, and the Yankees come the second day after they come through. I think I seed enough Yankees come through there to whup anything on God's earth. The Yankees camped three miles from our plantation at Mrs. Widow Sarah Saunders' across White Oak Creek on the Averysboro Road. Her son, Captain Ed Saunders, was in the Confederate Army. She was a big slave owner. She had about one hundred slaves. She was called a rich woman.

The Yankees played songs of "Walking the Streets of Baltimore," and "Walking in Maryland." They really played it. They slaughtered cows and sometimes only et the liver. I went to the camp after they left, and it was the awfulest stink I ever smelt in my life. They left them cows part of them lying where they were in the camp. They killed geese and chickens, and skinned them. Sometimes they skinned the hindquarters of a cow, cut them off, and left the rest.

When they told me I was free, I didn't notice it. I stayed on and worked just like I had been doing, right on with Missus and Master. I stayed there a year after the surrender.

I think some of the slaves was better off when they had owners and was in slavery than they is now. The colored people are slaves now more than they was then. I can show you wherein the nigger's got all his expenses to bear now. He gets his pay out'n the white man, and the white man don't pay him much. The nigger in the South is just as much a slave as ever. The nigger now is a better slave than when they owned him, 'cause he has his own expenses to bear. If you works a horse and don't have him to feed, you is better off than if you had to feed and care for him. That is the way that thing is now.

I think Mr. Roosevelt is a mighty nice man. He has done me a lot of good. No man can make times real good till everybody is put to work. With the land lying out there, can't be real good times. This is my illustration. My horse died last year. I ain't got no money to buy another and can't get one. You see that land lying out there; I have farmed it every year for a long time. Through part of the year, I always had vegetables and such to sell, but now my horse is dead, and I can't farm no more. I ain't got nothing to sell. I is bad out of heart. I sure hope something will be done for me.

Willis Cozart

Age 92 when interviewed
May 12, 1937, at Zebulon, N.C.,
by Mary A. Hicks

No MA'AM, MISTRESS, I don't want to ride in no automobile, thank you. I's done walked these three miles from Zebulon, and walking is what has kept me going all these years.

Yes'm, I's a bachelor, and I was borned on June 11, 1845, in Person County. Mr. Starling Oakley of Person County, near Roxboro, was my master, and as long as him and Old Mistress lived, I went back to see them.

He was right good to the good niggers and kinda strict with the bad ones. Personally, he ain't never have me whupped but two or three times. You's heard about these sit-down strikes lately; well, they ain't the first ones. Once, when I was four or five years old, too little to work in the fields, my master set me and some more little chilluns to work pulling up weeds around the house. Well, I makes a speech and I tells them, "Let's don't work none," so out we sprawls on the grass under the apple tree. After awhile, Old Master found us there, and when he finds that I was the ringleader, he gives me a little whupping.

It was a big plantation, 'round twelve hundred acres of land, I reckon, and he had about seventy or eighty slaves to work the cotton, corn, tobacco, and the wheat and vegetables. The big house was something to look at, but the slave cabins was just log huts with sand floors, and stick-and-dirt chimneys. We was allowed to have a little patch of garden stuff at the back, but no chickens nor pigs. The only way we had of making money was by picking berries and selling them. We ain't had much time to do that, 'cause we worked from sunup till sundown six days a week.

The master fed us as good as he knowed how, but it was mostly on bread, meat, and vegetables.

I remembers several slave sales where they sold the pappy or the mammy away from the chilluns, and that was a sad time. They led them up one at the time and asked them questions. And they warn't many what was chained, only the bad ones, and sometime when they was traveling it was necessary to chain a new gang.

I's seed niggers beat till the blood run, and I's seed plenty more with big scars, from whuppings, but they was the bad ones. You was whupped according to the deed you done in them days. A moderate whupping was thirty-nine or forty lashes, and a real whupping was a even hundred; most folks can't stand a real whupping.

From all this you might think that we ain't had no good times, but we had our cornshuckings, candypullings, and suchlike. We ain't felt like hunting much, but I did go on a few fox hunts with the master. I used to go fishing too, but I ain't been now since 1873, I reckon. We sometimes went to the neighborhood affairs, if'n we was good, but if we wasn't and didn't get a pass, the pattyrollers would sure get us. When they got through whupping a nigger, he knowed he was whupped, too.

The slave weddings in that country was sorta this way: The man asked the master for the woman, and he just told them to step over the broom, and that was the way they got married them days; the poor white folks done the same way.

After the war started, the white folks tried to keep us niggers from knowing about it, but the news got around somehow, and there was some talk of getting shut of the master's family and getting rich. The plans didn't amount to nothing, and so the Yankees come down.

I remembers mighty well when the Yankees come through our country. They stole everything they could find, and I remembers what Old Master said. He says, "Everyone that wants to work for me, get in the patch to pulling that forty acres of fodder, and all that don't, get up the road with them d——Yankees." Well, we all went away.

That winter was tough, all the niggers near about starved to death, and we ain't seed nothing of the forty acres of land and the mule what the Yankees done promise us neither. After awhile we had to go to our old masters and ask them for bread to keep us alive.

The Ku Klux Klan sprung right up out of the earth, but the Yankees put a stop to that by putting so many of them in jail. They do say that that's what the State Prison was built for.

I never believed in witches, and I ain't put much stock in haunts, but I's seed a few things during my life that I can't explain, like the thing with the red eyes that mocked me one night; but shucks, I ain't believing in them things much. I's plowed my land, tended it year after year, lived by myself and all, and I ain't got hurted yet, but I ain't never rid in a automobile yet, and I got one tooth left.

♦ ♦ ♦

W. L. Bost

Age 87 when interviewed
September 27, 1937
at 63 Curve Street, Asheville, N.C.,
by Marjorie Jones

MY MASSAS NAME WAS Jonas Bost. He had a
hotel in Newton, North Carolina. My mother
and grandmother both belonged to the Bost family.
My old massa had two large plantations, one about
three miles from Newton and another four miles
away. It took a lot of niggers to keep the work
a-going on them both. The women folks had to
work in the hotel and in the big house in town. Old
Missus, she was a good woman. She never allowed
the massa to buy or sell any slaves. There never was
an overseer on the whole plantation. The oldest
colored man always looked after the niggers. We
niggers lived better than the niggers on the other
plantations.

Lord, child, I remember when I was a little boy,
about ten years, the speculators come through Newton with droves of slaves. They always stay at our
place. The poor critters nearly froze to death. They
always come along on the last of December, so that
the niggers would be ready for sale on the first day
of January. Many the time I see four or five of them
chained together. They never had enough clothes
on to keep a cat warm. The women never wore
anything but a thin dress and a petticoat and one

79

underwear. I've seen the ice balls hanging on to the bottom of their dresses as they ran along, just like sheep in a pasture before they are sheared. They never wore any shoes. Just run along on the ground, all spewed up with ice. The speculators always rode on horses and drove the poor niggers. When they get cold, they make them run till they are warm again.

The speculators stayed in the hotel and put the niggers in the quarters just like droves of hogs. All through the night I could hear them mourning and praying. I didn't know the Lord would let people live who were so cruel. The gates were always locked and they was a guard on the outside to shoot anyone who tried to run away. Lord, Miss, them slaves look just like droves of turkeys running along in front of them horses.

I remember when they put them on the block to sell them. The ones between eighteen and thirty always bring the most money. The auctioneer, he stand off at a distance and cry them off as they stand on the block. I can hear his voice as long as I live.

If the one they going to sell was a young Negro man, this is what he say: "Now, gentlemen and fellow citizens, here is a big black buck Negro. He's stout as a mule. Good for any kind of work, and he never gives any trouble. How much am I offered for him?" And then the sale would commence, and the nigger would be sold to the highest bidder.

If they put up a young nigger woman, the auctioneer cry out: "Here's a young nigger wench, how much am I offered for her?" The poor thing stand on the block a-shivering and a-shaking nearly froze to death. When they sold, many of the poor mothers beg the speculators to sell them with their husbands, but the speculator only take what he want. So maybe the poor thing never see her husband again.

Old Massa always see that we get plenty to eat. Of course, it was no fancy rations. Just corn bread, milk, fat meat, and molasses, but the Lord knows that was lots more than other poor niggers got. Some of them had such bad massas.

Us poor niggers never allowed to learn anything. All the reading they ever hear was when they was carried through the big Bible. The massa say that keep the slaves in they places. They was one nigger boy in Newton who was terrible smart. He learn to read and write. He take other colored children out in the fields and teach them about the Bible, but they forget it before the next Sunday.

Then the pattyrollers, they keep close watch on the poor niggers so they have no chance to do anything or go anywhere. They just like policemen, only worser. Because they never let the niggers go anywhere without a pass from his massa. If you wasn't in your proper place when the pattyrollers come, they lash you till you was black and blue. The women got fifteen lashes and the men thirty. That is for just being out without a pass. If the nigger done anything worse, he was taken to the jail and put in the whipping post. They was two holes cut for the arms stretched up in the air and a block to put your feet in, then they whip you with cowhide whip. And the clothes sure never get any of them licks.

I remember how the driver, he was the man who did most of the whipping, use to whip some of the niggers. He would tie their hands together and then put their hands down over their knees, then take a stick and stick it between they hands and knees.

Then when he take hold of them and beat them, first on one side then on the other.

Plenty of the colored women have children by the white men. She know better than to not do what he say. Didn't have much of that until the men from South Carolina come up here and settle and bring slaves. Then they take them very same children what have they own blood and make slaves out of them. If the missus find out, she raise revolution. But she hardly find out. The white men not going to tell, and the nigger women were always afraid to. So they just go on hoping that thing won't be that way always.

Us niggers never have chance to go to Sunday school and church. The white folks feared for niggers to get any religion and education, but I reckon something inside just told us about God and that there was a better place hereafter. We would sneak off and have prayer meeting. Sometimes the patty-rollers catch us and beat us good, but that didn't keep us from trying. I remember one old song we use to sing when we meet down in the woods back of the barn. My mother, she sing and pray to the Lord to deliver us out of slavery. She always say she thankful she was never sold from her children, and that our massa not so mean as some of the others. But the old song, it went something like this:

Oh, Mother, let's go down,
Let's go down, let's go down, let's go down.
Oh, Mother, let's go down, down in the valley
   to pray.
As I went down in the valley to pray
Studying about that good old way,
Who shall wear that starry crown?
Good Lord, show me the way.

Then the other part was just like that, except it said "father" instead of "mother," and then "sister" and then "brother."

Then they sing sometimes:

We camp awhile in the wilderness,
In the wilderness, in the wilderness;
We camp awhile in the wilderness,
Where the Lord makes me happy,
And then I'm a-going home!

I don't remember much about the war. There was no fighting done in Newton. Just a skirmish or two. Most of the people get everything just ready to run when the Yankee soldiers come through the town. This was toward the last of the war. Course the niggers knew what all the fighting was about, but they didn't dare say anything. The man who owned the slaves was too mad as it was, and if the niggers say anything, they get shot right then and there. The soldiers tell us after the war that we get food, clothes, and wages from our massas, else we leave. But they was very few that ever got anything. Our old masssa say he not going pay us anything, 'cause his money was no good, but he wouldn't pay us if it had been.

Then after the war was over, we was afraid to move. Just like terrapins or turtles after emancipation. Just stick our heads out to see how the land lay. My mammy stay with Marse Jonah for about a year after freedom, then old Solomon Hall made her an offer. Old man Hall was a good man if there ever was one. My mother went to live on the place belonging to the nephew of Solomon Hall. All of her six children went with her. Mother, she cook for the white folks, and the children make crop.

When the first year was up, us children got the first money we had in our lives. My mother certainly was happy.

Then the Ku Klux Klan come along. They were terrible dangerous. They wear long gowns, touch the ground. They ride horses through the town at night, and if they find a Negro that tries to get nervy or have a little bit for himself, they lash him nearly to death and gag him and leave him to do the best he can. Sometime they put sticks in the top of the tall thing they wear and then put an extra head up there with scary eyes and great big mouth, then they stick it clear up in the air to scare the poor Negroes to death.

They had another thing they call the Donkey Devil that was just as bad. They take the skin of a donkey and get inside of it and run after the poor Negroes. Oh, Miss, them was bad times, them was bad times. I know folks think the books tell the truth, but they sure don't. Us poor niggers had to take it all.

When I was about twenty year old, I married a girl from West Virginia, but she didn't live but just about a year. I stayed down there for a year or so, and then I met Mamie. We came here and both of us went to work, we work at the same place. We bought this little piece of ground about forty-two years ago. We gave $125 for it. We had to buy the lumber to build the house a little at a time, but finally we got the house done. It's been a good home for us and the children. We have two daughters and one adopted son. Both of the girls are good cooks. One of them lives in New Jersey and cooks in a big hotel. She and her husband come to see us about once a year. The other one is in Philadelphia. They both have plenty. But the adopted boy, he was part white. We took him when he was a small and did the best we could by him. He never did like to associate with colored people. I remember one time when he was a small child, I took him to town, and the conductor made me put him in the front of the street car because he thought I was just caring for him and that he was a white boy. Well, we sent him to school until he finished. Then he joined the Navy. I ain't seen him in several years. The last letter I got from him, he say he ain't spoke to a colored girl since he has been there. This made me mad, so I took his insurance policy and cashed it. I didn't want nothing to do with him, if he deny his own color.

Very few of the Negroes ever get anywhere; they never have no education. I knew one Negro who got to be a policeman in Salisbury once, and he was a good one, too.

When my next birthday comes in December, I will be eighty-eight years old. That is, if the Lord lets me live, and I sure hope He does.

◆ ◆ ◆

Bibliography

My primary research source was the Federal Writers' Project collection, *Slave Narratives: A Folk History of Slavery in the U.S. from Interviews with Former Slaves*. The original manuscript of this collection is housed in the Rare Book and Special Collections Division of the Library of Congress. Facsimile editions of the collection are available. One edition was published by Scholarly Press of St. Clair Shores, Michigan in 1976. Another edition, entitled *The American Slave: A Composite Autobiography* and edited by George P. Rawick, was published by Greenwood Press of Westport, Connecticut in 1972. The latter edition also includes narratives from the Fisk University interviews of the 1920s as well as an original survey volume by the editor.

—B.H.

Other Narratives, Journals, and First-Person Accounts

Feelings, Tom. *To Be a Slave.* New York: Dial, 1968.
Jones, Thomas H. *The Experience of Thomas H. Jones, Who Was a Slave for Forty-Three Years.* New Bedford, N.Y.: E. Anthony & Sons, Ptrs., 1871.

Kemble, Fanny. *Journal of a Residence on a Georgian Plantation in 1838–1839*. New York: Harper & Row, 1863.

Killion, Ronald, and Charles Waller, eds. *Slavery Time*. Savannah, Ga.: Leehive Press, 1973.

Olmsted, Frederick Law. *A Journey in the Seaboard Slave Sates*. New York: Dix & Edwards, 1856.

Sterling, Dorothy. *The Trouble They Seen*. New York: Doubleday, 1976.

Yetman, Norman R. *Voices from Slavery*. New York: Holt, Rinehart and Winston, 1970.

Works by Historians and Scholars

Basset, J.S. *Slavery in the State of North Carolina*. Baltimore: Johns Hopkins Press, 1899.

Botkin, B.A. *Lay My Burden Down*. Univ. of Chicago Press, 1945.

Escott, Paul D. *Slavery Remembered*. Chapel Hill, N.C.: Univ. of North Carolina Press, 1979.

Gara, Larry. *Liberty Line: The Legend of the Underground Railroad*. Univ. of Kentucky Press, 1961.

Hamilton, J.G. de Roulhac. *Reconstruction in North Carolina*. Raleigh, N.C.: Presses of Edwards & Broughton, 1906.

Higginbotham, A. Leon Jr. *In the Matter of Color, Race, and the American Legal Process*. Oxford Univ. Press, 1978.

Rice, C. Duncan. *The Rise and Fall of Black Slavery*. New York: Harper & Row, 1975.

Rose, Willie Lee. *A Documentary History of Slavery in North America*. Oxford Univ. Press, 1976.

Scott, John Anthony. *Hard Trials on My Way*. New York: Knopf, 1974.

Siebert, Wilbur H. *The Underground Railroad from Slavery to Freedom*. 1898. Reprint. Arno Press, 1968.

Williamson, Joel. *After Slavery*. Chapel Hill: Univ. of North Carolina Press, 1965.

Zuber, Richard L. *North Carolina during Reconstruction*. Raleigh, N. C.: Dept. of Cultural Resources, Division of Archives and History, 1975.

◆ ◆ ◆

Before Freedom, When I Just Can Remember

Twenty-seven Oral Histories of Former South Carolina Slaves

For Joanne Bailey Wilson

Contents

Violet Guntharpe

Age 82, when interviewed by
W. W. Dixon, in Winnsboro, S.C.

I WAS BORN A slave in the Rocky Mount part of Fairfield County, up close to Great Falls. I hear them falls a-roaring now, and I see them waters flashing in the sunshine when I close my eyes.

My pappy name Robert and my mammy name Phyllis. They belong to the old-time aristocrats, the Gaither family. Does you know Miss Mattie Martin, which was the secretary of Governor Ansel? That one of my young missuses [also referred to as "mistress" and "old miss" in the *Slave Narratives*] and another is that pretty red-headed girl in the telegraph office at Winnsboro, that just sit there and pass out lightning and electricity over the wires wheresomever she take a notion. Before their mama marry Marster Starke Martin, her was Sally Gaither, my young missus in slavery time. Her die and go to Heaven last year, please God.

Marster Richard was a good marster [master; also referred to as "massa," "Maussa," "mass," and "marse"] to his slaves, though he took no foolishness and worked you from sun to sun. 'Spect him had about ten family of slaves and about fifty big and little slaves altogether on that plantation before them Yankees come and make a mess out of their lives.

95

Honey, us wasn't ready for the big change that come. Us had no education, no land, no mule, no cow, not a pig, nor a chicken, to set up housekeeping. The birds had nests in the air, the foxes had holes in the ground, and the fishes had beds under the great falls, but us colored folks was left without any place to lay our heads.

The Yankees sure throwed us in the briar patch, but us not bred and born there like the rabbit. Us born in a good log house. The cows was down there in the canebrakes to give us milk; the hogs was fattening on hickory nuts, acorns, and shucked corn to give us meat and grease; the sheep with their wool and the cotton in the gin house was there to give us clothes. The horses and mules was there to help that corn and cotton, but when them Yankees come and take all that away, all us had to thank them for, was a hungry belly, and Freedom. Something us had no more use for then, than I have today for one of them airplanes I hears flying round the sky, right now.

Well, after ravaging the whole countryside, the army got across old Catawba and left the air full of the stink of dead carcasses and the sky black with turkey buzzards. The white women was weeping in hushed voices, the niggers on the place not knowing what to do next, and the pickaninnies sucking their thumbs for want of something to eat. Mind you 'twas wintertime too.

Lots of the chillun die, as did the old folks, while the rest of us scour the woods for hickory nuts, acorns, cane roots, and artichokes, and seine the river for fish. The worst nigger men and women follow the army. The balance settle down with the white folks and simmer in their misery all through the springtime, till plums, mulberries, and blackberries come, and the shad come up the Catawba River.

My mammy stay on with the same marster till I was grown, that is fifteen, and Thad got to looking at me, meek as a sheep and dumb as a calf. I had to ask that nigger right out what his intentions was, before I get him to bleat out that he love me. Him name Thad Guntharpe.

I glance at him one day at the pigpen when I was slopping the hogs. I say, "Mr. Guntharpe, you follows me night and morning to this pigpen; do you happen to be in love with one of these pigs? If so, I'd like to know which one 'tis. Then sometime I come down here by myself and tell that pig about your affections."

Thad didn't say nothing but just grin. Him took the slop bucket out of my hand and look at it, all round it, put upside down on the ground, and set me down on it. Then, he fall down there on the grass by me and blubber out and warm my fingers in his hands.

I just took pity on him and told him mighty plain that he must limber up his tongue and ask something, say what he mean, wanting to visit them pigs so often.

Us carry on foolishness about the little boar shoat pig and the little sow pig, then I squeal in laughter. The slop bucket tipple over and I lost my seat. That ever remain the happiest minute of my eighty-two years.

After us marry, us moved on the Johnson place and Thad plow right on a farm where there use to be a town of Grimkeville. I was lonely down there all the time. I's halfway scared to death of the skeeters about my legs in daytime and old Captain Thorn's ghost in the nighttime.

You never heard about that ghost? If you went to school to Mr. Luke Ford sure he must of tell you about the time a slave boy killed his marster, Old Captain Thorn. He drag and throwed his body in the river.

When they find his body, they catch John, the slave boy, give him a trial by six white men, find him guilty, and he confess. Then, they took the broad axe, cut off his head, mount it on a pole, and stick it up on the bank where they find Old Captain Thorn.

That pole and head stay there till it rot down. Captain Thorn's ghost appear and disappear along that river bank ever since. My pappy tell me he see it and see the boy's ghost, too.

The ghost rode the minds of many colored folks. Some say that the ghost had a heap to do with deaths on that river, by drowning. One sad thing happen: the ghost and the malaria run us off the river.

Us moved to Marster Starke P. Martin's place. Him was a-setting at a window in the house one night, and somebody crept up there and fill his head full of buckshot. Marster Starke was Miss Sallie's husband, and Miss Mattie and Miss May's papa. Oh, the misery of that night to my white folks! Who did it? God knows! They sent poor Henry Nettles to the penitentiary for it, but most white folks and all the colored didn't believe he done it. White folks say a white man done it, but our color knew it was the work of that slave boy's ghost.

Did you ever read about foots of ghosts? They got foots and can jump and walk. No, they don't run. Why? 'Cause seem like their foots is too big. That night Marster Starke Martin was killed it was a-snowing. The whole earth was covered with a white blanket. It snowed and snowed and snowed. Us measure how big that snow was next morning and how big that ghost track.

The snow was seven inches and a little bit deep. The ghost track on top the snow big as a elephant's. Him or she or its tracks appear to drop with the snow and just rise up out the snow and disappear. The white folks say 'twas a man with bags on his foots, but they never found the bags, so I just believe it was ghost instigated by the devil to drop down there and make all that misery for my white folks.

My white folks come here from Maryland, I heard them say. They fought in the Revolution, set up a tanyard when they got here, and then when cotton come, my marster's pappy was the first to put up a horse-gin and screw pit in Rocky Mount section. I glories in their blood, but there's none by the name around here now, 'cept colored folks.

There's a great day a-coming, when the last trumpet will sound and the devil and all the ghosts will be chained and they can't romp around the old river and folks' houses in the nighttime and bring sorrow and pain in the wake of them big tracks.

Brawley Gilmore

Interviewed by Caldwell Sims at
34 Hamlet Street, Union, S.C.;
December 1936

W E LIVED IN A log house during the Ku Klux
days. They would watch you just like a chicken
rooster watching for a worm. At night, we was
scared to have a light. They would come around
with the "dough faces" on, and peer in the windows, and open the door. If you didn't look out,
they would scare you half to death.

John Good, a darky blacksmith, used to shoe the
horses for the Ku Klux. He would mark the horse-
shoes with a bent nail or something like that; then
after a raid, he could go out in the road and see if a
certain horse had been rode. So, he began to tell on
the Ku Klux.

As soon as the Ku Klux found out they was being
give away, they suspicioned John. They went to him
and made him tell how he knew who they was.
They kept him in hiding; and when he told his
tricks, they killed him.

When I was a boy on the Gilmore place, the Ku
Klux would come along at night a-riding the niggers
like they was goats. Yes, sir, they had them down
on all-fours a-crawling, and they would be on their
backs. They would carry the niggers to Turk Creek
bridge and make them set up on the bannisters of

the bridge. Then, they would shoot them offen the bannisters into the water. I declare them was the awfulest days I ever is seed.

A darky name Sam Scaife drifted a hundred yards in the water downstream. His folks took and got him outen that bloody water and buried him on the bank of the creek. The Ku Klux would not let them take him to no graveyard. Fact is, they would not let many of the niggers take the dead bodies of the folks nowhere. They just throwed them in a big hole right there and pulled some dirt over them. For weeks after that, you could not go near that place, because it stink so far and bad.

Sam's folks, they throwed a lot of "Indian-head" rocks all over his grave, 'cause it was so shallow, and them rocks kept the wild animals from a-bothering Sam. You can still see them rocks. I could carry you there right now.

Another darky, Eli McCollum, floated about three-and-a-half miles down the creek. His folks went there and took him out and buried him on the banks of the stream right by the side of a Indian mound. You can see that Indian mound to this very day. It is big as my house is, over there on the Chester side.

The Ku Klux and the niggers fit at New Hope Church. A big rock marks the spot today. The church, it done burnt down. The big rock sets about seven miles east of Lockhart on the road to Chester. The darkies killed some of the Ku Klux and they took their dead and put them in Pilgrims' Church. Then, they set fire to that church and it burnt everything up to the very bones of the white folks. And ever since then, that spot has been known as Burnt Pilgrim. The darkies left most of the folks right there for the buzzards and other wild things to eat up. Because them niggers had to get away from there; and they didn't have no time for to fetch no word or nothing to no folks at home.

They had a hiding place not far from Burnt Pilgrim. A darky name Austin Sanders, he was carrying some victuals to his son. The Ku Klux catch him and they asked him where he was a-going. He allowed that he was a-setting some bait for coons. The Ku Klux took and shot him and left him lying right in the middle of the road with a biscuit in his dead mouth.

Dr. McCollum was one of them Ku Klux, and the Yankees set out for to catch him. Doc, he rid a white pony called Fannie. Doc, he liked to fiddle. Old Fannie, she would get up on her hind legs when the doc would play his fiddle. All the darkies, they love Doc, so they would help him for to get away from the Yankees, even though he was a Ku Klux.

It's one road what forks, after you cross Woods Ferry. Don't nobody go over that old road now. One fork go to Leeds and one to Chester. Well, right in this fork, Mr. Buck Worthy had done built him a grave in the Woods Ferry Graveyard.

It was built out of marble and it was covered up with a marble slab. Mr. Worthy, he would take and go there and open it up and get in it on pretty days.

So old Doc, he knowed about that grave. He was going to see a sick lady one night when some Yankees got after him. He was on old Fannie. They was about to catch the old Doc when he reached in sight of that graveyard. It was dark. So Doc, he drive the horse on past the fork, and then he stop and hitch her in front of some dense pines.

Then, he went to that grave, slip that top slab back, got in there, and pulled it over him, just leaving a little crack. Doc allowed he wrapped up hisself in his horse blanket, and when the Yankees left, he went to sleep in that grave and never even woke up till the sun, it was a-shining in his face.

Soon after that, my sister took down sick with the misery. Doc, he come to see her at night. He would hide in the woods in daytime. We would fetch him his victuals. My sister was sick three weeks before she died. Doc, he would take some blankets and go and sleep in that grave, 'cause he knowed they would look in our house for him. They kept on a-coming to our house. Course, we never knowed nothing about no doctor at all.

There was a nigger with wooden bottom shoes, that stuck to them Yankees and other poor white trash around there. He allowed with his big mouth that he going to find the doctor. He told it that he had seed Fannie in the graveyard at night.

Us heard it and told the doctor. Us did not want him to go near that graveyard anymore. But Doc, he just laugh and he allowed that no nigger was a-going to look in no grave, 'cause he had tried to get me to go over there with him at night and I was scared.

One night, just as Doc was a-covering up, he heard them wooden shoes a-coming. So, he sat up in the grave and took his white shirt and put it over his head. He seed three shadows a-coming. Just as they got near the doc, the moon come out from behind a cloud and Doc, he wave that white shirt, and he say them niggers just fell over gravestones a-getting out of that graveyard. Doc allowed that he heard them wooden shoes a-going up the road for three miles. Well, they never did bother the doctor anymore.

Hester Hunter

*Age 85, when interviewed by
Annie Ruth Davis, in Marion, S.C.;
May 1937.*

R EMEMBER THE FIRST TIME them Yankees come.
I was sitting down in the chimney corner and
my mammy was giving me my breakfast. Remember I been sitting there with my milk and my bowl
of hominy, and I hear my old grandmammy come
a-running in from out the yard and say all the sky
was blue as indigo with the Yankees coming right
there over the hill. Say she see more Yankees than
could ever cover up all the premises about there.

Then, I hear my missus scream and come a-running with a lapful of silver and tell my grandmammy
to bury and sew that up in the feather bed, 'cause
them Yankees was mighty apt to destroy all they
valuables. Old Missus tell all the colored people to
get away, get away and take care of themselves,
and tell we children to get back to the chimney
corner, 'cause she couldn't protect us noways, no
longer.

I remember I hear tell that my old stepfather
been gone to the mill to grind some corn, and when
he was coming down the road, two big Yankees
jump out the bushes side the road and tell him stop
there. He say they tell him if he want to save his
neck, he better get off that ox right then and get

away from there. He say he been so scared he make for the woods fast as he could get there, and tell that he lay down with knots under his head many a night before he would venture to come out from that woods. Never hear tell of his ox and corn no more neither.

I remember my boss had one of my old missus' niggers up there in the yard one morning and say he was going whip him, and my missus say, "John C., you let my nigger alone." You see, my missus had her niggers and then Old Boss had his niggers, 'cause when Old Missus been marry Marster John C. Bethea, she had brought her share of niggers from where she was raised in the country.

It been like this, Old Missus' father had scratched the pen for every one of his chillun to have so many niggers apiece for they portion of his property, so long as they would look after them and treat them good. Then, if there been talk that them chillun never do what he say do, they was to take them niggers right back to they old marster home. But, child, they never didn't take no niggers away from my old missus, 'cause she sure took care of them. Stuck to her niggers till she died.

I remember just as good there been two long row of nigger house up in the quarter, and the Bethea niggers been stay in the row on one side, and the Davis niggers been stay in the row on the other side. And, honey, there been so much difference in the row on this side and the row on that side. My God, child, you could go through there and spot the Sara Davis niggers from the Bethea niggers time you see them.

All Old Missus' niggers had they brush pile side they house to sun they beds on and dry they washing, 'cause my missus would see to it herself that they never kept no nasty living. We was raise decent, honey, and that howcome me and my chillun is that way to this very day.

No, ma'am, ain't nobody never didn't turn no key on me. I remember, if my old missus would hear talk that we been bother something that didn't belong to us, she would whip us and say, "I'm not mad, but you chillun have got to grow up some day. You might have to suffer worse than this, if you don't learn better while you young."

Them niggers what been bred on Marster John C. Bethea's plantation never know nothing but big living in that day and time. Recollect that they would give all they colored people so much of flour for they Sunday eating, and then they had a certain woman on the place to cook all the other ration for the niggers in one big pot out in Old Marster's yard.

All the niggers would go there to the pot on Sunday and get they eating, like turnips and collards and meat, and carry it to they house and make they own bread. Then, in the weektime, they would come out the field at twelve o'clock and stand around the pot and eat they pan of ration, and then they would go back in the field and work.

When they would come home at night, there would be enough cooked up for them to carry home to last till the next day dinner. Didn't eat no breakfast no time. Had meat, greens, cornbread, and dumplings to eat mostly, and won't no end to milk.

Course, them what been stay to the white folks' house would eat to the missus' kitchen. And, my Lord, child, my white folks had the prettiest kind of rice that they made right there on they own plantation. Had plenty rice to last them from one year to the other, just like they had they hominy.

Then Old Marster had a big fish pond, and in the

summertime when it would get too hot to work, he would allow all his plantation niggers to catch all the pikes and jacks they wanted and salt them down in barrels for the winter. Din't allow nobody to go nowhere about that fish pond but us niggers.

And another thing, they wouldn't cure they meat with nothing but this here green hickory wood, and I speak about what I been know, there ain't never been nothing could touch the taste of them hams and shoulder meat. Oo-oo-oo, honey, they would make the finest kind of sausages in them days. I tell my chillun I just about turn against these sausage the people make about here these days.

Oh, the people, they is awful worser than what they used to be. I know by my coming on that they awful worser. The little tots about here these days know things the older people used to be the only ones that know about. I does worry about it so much. Sometimes, child, I goes along just a-whistling "Lord, I wish I had went before I had so much to grieve over."

♦ ♦ ♦

Ben Horry

*Age 87, when interviewed by
Genevieve W. Chandler,
in Murrells Inlet, S.C.; August 1937.*

I THE OLDEST LIVER left on Waccamaw Neck, that belong to Brookgreen, Prospect, Longwood, Alderly plantations. I been here! I seen thing! I tell you. That woods you see been Colonel Josh Ward's taters patch. Right to Brookgreen Plantation where I born.

They say Colonel Ward the biggest rice man been on Waccamaw. He start that big gold rice in the country. He the head rice captain in them time. My father, the head man, he tote the barn key. Rice been money, them day and time.

My father love he liquor. That take money. He ain't have money, but he have the rice barn key and rice been money. So my father gone in woods, take a old stump, have 'em hollow out. Now he same as mortar [used for separating seed from husk] to the barnyard. And my father keep a pestle hide handy. Hide two pestle! Them pestle make outer heart pine. When that pestle been missed, I wasn't know nothing.

The way I knows my age, when the slavery-time war come, I been old enough to go in the woods with my father and hold a lightwood torch for him to see to pestle off that golden rice he been tote out the barn and hide. *That* rice he been take to town Saturday when the Colonel and my father go to get provision, like sugar, coffee, pepper, and salt. With the money he get when he sell that rice, he buy liquor. He been hide that sack of rice before day clean, in the prow of the boat, and cover with a thing like an old coat.

I remembers one day when he come back from town he make a miss when he unloading and fell and broke he jug. The big boss see; he smell; and he see why my father make that miss step. He already sample that liquor. But the boss ain't say too much.

Saturday time come to ration off. Every head on the plantation to Brookgreen line up at smokehouse to draw he share of meat, rice, grits, and meal. (This was before my father been appointed head man. This when they had a tight colored man in that place by name Fraser. They say Fraser com straight from Africa.)

Well, Saturday, when time come to give my father he share of rations, the head man reach down in the corner and pull out a piece of that broke whiskey jug and put on top my father rations where all could see. Colonel Ward cause that to be done to broke him off from that whiskey jug. My father was a steady liquor man till then, and the boss broke him off.

Slavery going in. I remembers Marster Josh and Miss Bess had come from French Broad where they summered it. They brought a great deal of this cloth they call blue drilling to make a suit for every boy big enough to wear a suit of clothes and a pair of shoes for every one. I thought *that* the happiest setup I had in boyhood. Blue drilling pants and coat and shoe. And Sunday come, we have to go to the big house for Marster Josh to see how the clothes fit. And him and Miss Bess make us run races to see who run the fastest. That the happiest time I remembers when I was a boy to Brookgreen.

Two Yankee gunboats come up Waccamaw River. Come by us plantation. One stop to Sandy Island, Montarena Landing. One gone Wachesaw Landing. Old Marster Josh and all the white buckra [Gullah dialect for white person] gone to Marlboro County to hide from Yankee. Gone up Waccamaw River and up Pee Dee River, to Marlboro County, in a boat by name *Pilot Boy*. Take Colonel Ward and all the Captain to hide from gunboat till peace declared. I think *Pilot Boy* been a rear-wheeler. Most boats like the *Old Planter* been side-wheeler.

They say the Yankee broke in all the rice barn on Sandy Island and share the rice out to colored people. The big mill to Laurel Hill been burn right then. That the biggest rice mill on Waccamaw River. Twasn't the Yankee burn them mill. These white mens have a idea the Yankee mean to burn these mill so they set 'em afire before the Yankee come. Nothing left to Laurel Hill today but the rice mill tower. That old brick tower going to *be* there. Fire can't harm 'em.

The worst thing I remembers was the colored overseer. He was the one straight from Africa. He the boss over all the mens and womens, and if womans don't do all he say, he lay task on 'em they ain't able to do. My mother won't do all he say. When he say, "You go barn and stay till I come," she ain't do 'em. So, he have it in for my mother and lay task on 'em she ain't able for do.

Then, for punishment, my mother is take to the barn and strapped down on thing called The Pony. Hands spread like this and strapped to the floor and all two both she feet been tied like this. And she been give twenty-five to fifty lashes till the blood flow. And my father and me stand right there and look and ain't able to lift a hand! Blood on floor in that rice barn when barn tear down by Huntington.

If Marster Josh been know about that overseer, the overseer can't do em, but just the house servant get Marster Josh and Miss Bess ear. Them things different when my father been make the head man. What I tell you happen before Freedom, when I just can remember.

Father dead just before my mother. They stayed right to Brookgreen Plantation and dead there after they free. And all they chillun do the same, till the old colonel sell the plantation out. Where we going to? Ain't we got house and rations there?

After Freedom, from my behavior with my former owner, I was appointed head man on Brookgreen Plantation. When canal been dug out from the Oaks Plantation to Dr. Wardie C. Flagg house, I was appointed head man. Canal cut 1877. Near as I can, I must task it on the canal and turn in every man's work to Big Boss. That canal bigger than one Mr. Huntington dig right now with machine.

More than one storm I live through. Been through the Flagg storm. Been turned over twice outside there in the sea. One time been have the seine. Been rough. Have weather. And the breakers take the boat. I swim till I get the rope hold. Two men on the shore have the rope end of the seine rope and I hold to that, and that how I save that time.

'Member another time. Had a boat full of people this last go-round. Was Miss Mary, her aunty, and lawyer. I take them fishing outside in ocean. Been in the inlet mouth. Come halfway to Drunken Jack Island. Breaker start to lick in the boat. I start to bail. Have a tomato can for bail with. And that been dangerous, have too much women in there; they couldn't swim like a man. And it happen by accident, when the boat swamp and full with water, our *feet touch bottom*. When he turn over, I didn't aim to do nothing but swim for myself. Wasn't able to help nobody. But here our feet touch bottom. Only an accident from God!

One time again I swamp outside, 'tween Georgetown and Charleston. Try to bail. Swim with one hand, hold boat with the other. Roughest time I ever see 'cause it been cold weather. Old beforetime yawl boat, carry eight oar, four to each side. Young man then—1877. After the weather surrender, we gone back in there and find cork going up and down and save us net and all.

When the Flagg storm been, 1893, I working for Ravanel and Holmes. I was taken up in that storm in a steamer boat. Leave Charleston generally about five in morning. That trip never reach Georgetown till nine that night. Meet a man on that trip got he wife hugged to mast in a little kinder lifeboat. Had he two chillun, rope wrap 'em to that mast. Save man and wife and chillun, and gone back, and save he trunk. After that, they quit call me Ben; they call me Rooster.

After Flagg storm, Colonel Ward take me and Peter Carr, us two and a horse, take that shore to Little River. Search for all them what been drowned. Find a trunk to Myrtle Beach. Have all kinder thing in 'em: comb for you hair, thing you put on you wrist. Find dead horse, cow, ox, turkey, fowl— everything. Gracious God! Don't want to see no more thing like that! But no dead body find on beach outside Flagg family.

Find two of them chillun way down to Dick Pond

what drownded to Magnolia Beach, find them in a distance apart from here to that house. All that family drown out, because they wouldn't go to this lady house on higher ground. Wouldn't let none of the rest go. Servant all drown. Betsy, Kit, Mom Adele. Couldn't identify who lost from who save till next morning. Find old Doctor body by he vest stick out of the mud. Fetch Doctor body to shore and he watch still a-ticking. Dr. Wardie Flagg been save hanging to a beach cedar. When that tornado come, my house wash down off he blocks. Didn't broke up.

Religion? Reckon Stella [his wife] got the morest of that. I sometimes a little quick. Stella, she holds one course. I like good song. One I like best,

> Try us, Oh Lord,
> And search the ground
> Of every sinful heart!
> Whate'er of sin
> In us be found,
> Oh, bid it all depart!

Make my living with the oyster. Before time, I get seventy-five cents a bushel; now I satisfy with fifty cents. Tide going out, I go out in a boat with the tide. Tide bring me in with sometimes ten, sometimes fifteen or twenty bushels. I make white folks a roast. White folks come to Uncle Ben from all over the country—Florence, Dillon, Mullins— every kind of place. Same price roast or raw, fifty cents a bushel.

Jake McLeod

Age 83, when interviewed by
Lucile Young and H. Grady Davis,
in Timmonsville, S.C.; August 1937

I BORN IN LYNCHBURG, South Carolina the thir-
teenth day of November 1854. Born on the
McLeod place. Grandparents born on the McLeod
place, too. My white folks, they didn't sell and buy
slaves; and that howcome my grandfather Riley
McLeod fell to Frank McLeod and Grandmother
fell to the McRaes.

My boss give my grandfather to his sister, Carolina, that had married the McRae, so they wouldn't
be separated. They take them and go to Florida,
and when the Yankees went to Florida, they hitched
up the teams and offered to bring them back to
South Carolina. Some of my uncles and aunts come
back, but my grandfather and grandmother stayed
in Florida till they died.

The McLeods, they was good people. Believe in
plenty work, eat and wear all the time, but work us
very reasonable. The overseer, he blow horn for us
to go to work at sunrise. Give us task to do, and if
you didn't do it, they put the little thing to you.
That was a leather lash or some kind of a whip.
Didn't have no whipping post in our neighborhood.

They didn't have no jails in them days, but I
recollects one woman hanged on the galleries

[gallows]. Hang them up by harness and broke neck for wrongdoing, like killing somebody or trying to kill. Old woman cooking for the Scotts, named Peggy, tried to poison the Scotts. Mean to her, she say, and she put poison in the coffee. My mother walked about ten miles to see that hanging, 'cause they turned the slaves loose to go to a hanging. Took her from the quarter in the wagon, and I heard her tell that the old lady, Peggy, was sitt1ng on her coffin. My mother say she used to use so much witchcraft, and someone whispered, "Why don't you do something about it?" She say, "It too late now." I hear tell about them hanging, but I ain't see none of it.

My boss had four slave house that was three or four hundred yards from his house, and I reckon he had about twenty-five slaves. One was pole house with brick chimney, and two rooms partitioned off; and the other three was clay house. Us had frame bed and slept on shucks and hay mattress.

They didn't give us no money, but had plenty to eat every day. Give us buttermilk, sweet potaoes, meat, and cornbread to eat mostly. Catch a nigger with wheat, they give him "wheat." Then, they let us have a garden and extra patches of we own that we work on Saturday evenings. And we catch as much rabbits and fish as us want. Catch pikes and eels and cats. Catch fish with hook and line in Lynches River with Senator E. D. Smith's father. The Reverend Bill Smith the father of E. D. Smith.

The white folks, they had a woman to each place to weave the cloth and make all us clothes. The women had to weave five cuts a week, one cut a night. Have reel in the shape of wheel. Spoke turn and hold thread and turn and when it click, it a cut. Any over, keep it to the next week.

They wore cotton clothes in the summer and wool

clothes in the winter, and had more than one garment, too. Had different clothes to wear on Sunday, 'cause the slaves go to the white folks' church in that day and time. Then, they had shoemaker to come there and make all the colored people's shoes. The Durant shoemaker come to the McLeod plantation and make they shoes.

I telling you my boss was a good man. He had a big plantation with six or seven hundred acres of land, but he didn't have to mind to see about none of the work. The overseer name Dennis, and he was the one to look out for all the plantation work. He lived on the McLeod place, and he was good man to us. I had to thin cotton and drop peas and corn, and I was a halfhand two years during the war. If a whole hand hoes one acre, then a halfhand hoes half a acre. That what a half-hand is.

Wheat, peas, corn, and cotton was the things that peoples plant mostly in them days. This how I see them frail the wheat out. Put pole in hard land and drive horse in circle and let them stamp it out. You could ride or walk. Two horses tramp and shake it out, and then take straws and have something to catch it in and wind it out. Had to pick and thrash a bushel of peas a day.

When corn-hauling time come, every plantation haul corn and put in circle in front of the barn. Have two piles and appoint two captains. They take sides and give corn shucking like that. Shuck corn and throw in front of door, and sometimes shuck corn all night. After they get through with the shucking, give big supper and march all around Old Marster's kitchen and house. Have tin pans, buckets, and canes for music and dance in front of the house in the road. Go to another place and help them shuck corn the next time, and so on that way.

My old missus and marster, they always look after they slaves when they get sick. Use herbs for they medicine. I used to know different herbs my mother would get. Boneset and life-everlasting make teas for fever and colds. When I was a boy, they used to carry them what have smallpox by the swamp and built a dirt house for them. Kept them there and somebody carried food to them. People used to have holes in they skin with that thing, and most of them died.

I hear tell about one man running away from Black Creek and going to Free State. Catch ride with people that used to travel to Charleston hauling cotton and things. He come back about fifteen years after the war and lived in that place adjoin to me. Come back with barrels and boxes of old secondhand clothes and accumulated right smart here. Talk good deal about how he associated with the whites. Don't know howcome he run away, but they didn't catch up with him till it was too late.

The community have man then called patroller [local slave patrol; also patteroller, pataroller, pattyroller, etc.], and they business was to catch them that run away. Say like you be authorized to look after my place, you catch them that slipped off to another man place. Couldn't leave off plantation to go to another place without you ask for a pass and have it on you.

White folks used to kill beef what they call "club beef." If you kill beef this week, you send this one and that one a piece till the beef all gone. White folks give me pass and tell me carry beef and deliver it. Next time, another man send us beef.

I run away one time. Somehow, the overseer know where I was. I recollects Old Missus had me tied to the tester bedstead, and she whip me till the whip broke. I see her getting another arm about full, and I tear loose and run away. I slip home on steps at my mother's house, looking down, playing with the cat, and look up in her face. She say, "You good-for-nothing, you get out of here and get to that barn and help them shuck corn."

I go, but I didn't go in, 'cause I keep a watch on her.

All I know about the war that bring Freedom was that the war was going on. I remember when they couldn't get coffee, sugar, or nothing like that. You know that was a tough time to think about; we couldn't get no salt. Cut up potatoes and parch to make coffee. Boil dirt out the smokehouse and put liquor in food. Eat pokeberry for greens. Then one day we hear gunfire in Charleston and Missus make miration [outcry].

I don't remember Freedom, but I know when we signed the contract, the Yankees give us to understand that we was free as our marster was. Couldn't write, just had to touch the pen. Ask us what name we wanted to go in.

We work on then, for one-third the crop the first year, with the boss furnishing everything. Soon as got little ahead, went to sharecropping.

I tell you, it been a pretty hard time to be up against. I own this here place, and my nephew live here with me. They give him government job with the understanding he help me. Get $24.80 a month and live off that. If carried out like the president want it carried out, it be better than slavery time. You know, some slaves got along mighty bad, 'cause most of the white people wasn't like our white folks.

Adeline Jackson

Age 88, when interviewed by
W. W. Dixon, in Winnsboro, S.C.

I WAS BORN FOUR miles southwest of where I is now, on the other side of Woodward Station. I was a slave of Old Marster John Mobley, the richest man, the largest landowner, and with more niggers than any other white man in the county. He was the seventh son of the seventh son, so he allowed, and you know that's a sign of a big family, lots of cows, mules, horses, money, chillun, and everything that's worth having.

He had a good wife, too. This the way he got her, he say. She the daughter of Old Major Andy McLean, who got a body full of bullets in the Revolution. The Old Major didn't want Katie to marry Marster John. Marster John git on a mule and ride up in the night. Miss Katie runned out, jump up behind him, run away, and marry Marster John.

They had the same birthday, March 27, but Marster John two years older than Miss Katie. That day was looked to, same as Christmas, every year that come. Big times then, I tell you!

My missus had long hair, touching the floor and could dance, so Marster John said, with a glass of water on top of her head.

Marster John got religion and went all the way,

like the jailer in the Bible. All the house joined with him and most of the slaves. It was Baptist, and he built a spanking good church building down the road, all out of his own money. The cemetery there yet. He called it Fellowship. Some fine tombstones in there yet. The finest cost two thousand dollars; that's his daughter Nancy's tomb. Marster John and my old missus buried in there.

When my youngest missus, name Marion Rebecca, married her second cousin, Marster Edward P. Mobley, I was give to her and went with them to the June place. It was called that because old Dr. June built it and sold it to Marster Ed. I nursed her first chillun: Edward, Moses Hill, John, and Katie.

It was a large, two-story frame house, with chimneys at each gable end. Marster Edward got to be as rich as Old Marster; he owned the June place, the Rochelle plantation, the Peay place, and the Roebuck place. Yes, sir, course us had overseers for so many slaves and plantations.

Slaves lived in quarters, a stretch of small houses off from the White House [often used in speaking of the master's house. Also Big House]. Patrollers often come to search for stray slaves, wouldn't take your word for it. They would search the house. If they catch one without a pass, they whipped him.

In course of time, I was took off the nursing and put to the field. I dropped cotton seed, hoed some, and picked cotton. I never learned to read or write.

At certain times we worked long and hard, and you had to be particular. The only whipping I got was for chopping down a good cornstalk near a stump in a new ground. When farm work was not pressing, we got all of Saturday to clean up around the houses, and wash and iron our clothes.

Marster Henry Gibson was our doctor. Yes,

women in family way worked up to near the time, but guess Dr. Gibson knowed his business. Just before the time, they was took out and put in the carding and spinning rooms.

Marster never sold a slave, but swaps were made with kinpeople to advantage, slaves' wives and husbands sometimes. Marster Edward bought a slave in Tennessee just 'cause he could play the fiddle. Named him Tennessee Ike, and he played along with Ben Murray, another fiddler. Sometime all of us would be called up into the front yard to play and dance and sing for Miss Marion, the chillun, and visitors. Everything lively at Christmas time, dances with fiddles, patting, and stick rattling; but when I joined the church, I quit dancing.

I went to White Poplar Springs Church, the Baptist church my missus attended. We got most our outside news Sunday at church. The preacher was Mr. Cartledge. He allowed Miss Marion was the flower of his flock.

Our neighbors was the Peays, the Durhams, the Picketts, the Barbers, and Boulwares. All these folks kept a pack of hounds to run deer and foxes. I has eat many pieces of deer.

After the war, a man came along on a red horse; he was dressed in a blue uniform and told us we was free. The Yankees that I remembers was not gentlefolks. They stole everything they could take. The meanest thing I ever see was shoats they half killed, cut off the hams, and left the other parts quivering on the ground.

I married Mose Jackson, after Freedom, and had a boy, Henry. Last I heard, he was at Shelby, North Carolina. My missus was a good Christian woman. She give me a big supper when I was married.

I was much happier them days than now. Maybe it won't be so bad when I gets my old age pension.

Adele Frost

Age 93, when interviewed by
Hattie Mobley, in Richland County, S.C.

I WAS BORN IN Adams Run, South Carolina, January 21, 1844. My father name was Robert King, and my mother was Minder King. My father was born in Adams Run, but my mother came from Spring Grove, South Carolina. My master was kind to his slaves, and his overseers was all Negroes. He had a large farm at Parker's Ferry.

I was brought here at the age of twelve to be maid for Mr. Mitchell, from who I didn't get any money, but a place to stay and plenty of food and clothes. I never gone to school in my life, and Marster nor Missus ever help me to read. I used to wear thin clothes in hot weather and warm, comfortable ones in the winter. On Sunday I wear a old-time bonnet, armhole apron, shoes, and stocking. My bed was the old-time four-post with pavilion [canopy] hanging over the top.

On the plantation was a meeting house in which we used to have meetings every Tuesday night, Wednesday night, and Thursday night. I used to attend the white church. Dr. Jerico was the pastor. Colored people had no preacher, but they had leader. Every slave go to church on Sunday, cause they didn't have any work to do for Marster. My grandma used to teach the catechism and how to sing. I joined the church 'cause I wanted to be a Christian, and I think everybody should be.

Funerals was at night, and when ready to go to the graveyard, everybody would light a lightwood knot as torch while everybody sing. This is one of the songs we used to sing:

> Going to carry this body
> To the graveyard,
> Graveyard, don't you know me?
> To lay this body down.

We ain't had no doctor. Our missus and one of the slaves would attend to the sick.

The Yankees take three nights to march through. I was afraid of them and climbed into a tree. One call me down and say, "I am your friend." He give me a piece of money and I wasn't afraid no more.

After the war, I still work as a maid for Mr. Mitchell.

My husband was Daniel Frost. We didn't have no wedding, just married at the judge office. We had three chillun.

I move here [near Columbia] with my granddaughter, about ten year ago.

◆ ◆ ◆

Milton Marshall

Age 82, when interviewed by
G. L. Summer, in Newberry, S.C., RFD;
September 1937

I LIVE IN NEWBERRY County, a few miles from town on Mr. Alan Johnstone's place. I rent and make a fair living. I have ten children now living and two dead. They is all on a farm. I was born in Union County, just across the Newberry line, near the Goshen Hill section. I was young when we moved to Newberry, and I have lived there nearly all my life. My father, Ned Worthy, was a slave of Frank Bynum's mother. My mother was Marla Worthy, who was a slave of Dr. Burton Maybin. She cooked for a long time for the Maybin family.

My grandfather was called Jack, and he was a nigger-driver. That was a nigger that had to oversee the slaves when the marster was away from home. He would call the cows like this: "Soo—ey, Soo—ey" or "Sook, Sook." He called his dogs by whistling. He had several dogs. There was many dogs on the farms, mostly hounds and bird dogs.

When grandpa died and was buried, his dogs would get out and bark and trail just like trailing a rabbit, and the trail always led to the graveyard. There they would stand by his grave and howl for a long time, with their heads up in the air.

The old folks made medicines from root herbs

124

and tree barks. Herb tea was made to keep away fevers. Marster always called his big chaps up to the house in the mornings and made them drink chinaberry tea to keep worms from getting in them. Many of the slaves, and some old white people, too, thought there was witches in them days. They believed a witch could ride you and stop blood circulation.

Marster Burt Maybin owned sixty-eight slaves, and I was one, and is the only one now living. We had no money in slavery time, just got food and clothes for our work. But my marster was a good feeder, always had enough to eat. Every Sunday he would give each nigger a quart of flour extra for breakfast. Some of the marsters didn't give niggers much to eat, and they had to slip off and steal.

We had plenty of what was the rule for eating in them days. We had homemade molasses, peas, cornbread, and home-raised meat sometimes. We killed rabbits and possums to eat, and sometimes went fishing and hunting.

Our clothes was made at home, spun and wove by the women folks. Copper straw and white cloth was used. Our shoes was made by a shoemaker in the neighborhood who was named Liles. They was made with wooden soles or bottoms. They tanned the leather or had it tanned in the neighborhood. It was tacked around the soles. It was rawhide leather, and the shoes had to be soaked in warm water and greased with tallow or meat skin so the shoes would slip on the feet.

All of us had to go to work at daylight and work till dark. They whipped us a little and they was strict about some things. Us chaps did not learn to read and write; that is why I can't read and write today. Marster wouldn't allow us to learn.

I was small in slavery time, and played with the white chaps. Once he saw me and some other chaps, white chaps, under a tree playing with letter blocks. They had the ABCs on them. Marster got awful mad and got off his horse and whipped me good.

Some of the slaves was whipped while they was tied to a stock. My marster was all right, but awful strict about two things: stealing and telling a lie. He sure whipped them if they was caught in them things.

We had to work all day Saturdays, but Marster wouldn't let anybody work on Sunday. Sometimes he would give the women part of Saturday afternoons so they could wash. He wouldn't allow fishing and hunting on Sundays either, unless it looked like rain and the fodder in the field had to be brought in. He always give us Christmas Day off, and we had lots of good eats then.

A stage that was drawn by two horses went past our place. It carried mail and people. When Marster wanted to send word to any people in the neighborhood, he sent it by somebody on a horse.

We had good white neighbors in slavery time. I remember the old corn shuckings, cotton-pickings, and logrollings. He would ask all the neighbors' hands in and they would come by crowds. I can remember them good.

I remember the grain was put in drains and the horses was made to tramp on it to get the seed out. Then, it was put in a house and poured in a big wooden fan machine, which fanned out the chaff. The machine was turned by two men.

They made molasses by taking the cane and squeezing out the juice in a big wooden machine. The machines now is different. They is made of cast.

The niggers didn't have a church on the planta-

tion but was made to go to the white folks' church
and set in back of the church. They had to get a
pass to go to church same as any other place, or the
patrollers would catch 'em and beat 'em.

After the war was over, the niggers built brush
arbors for to hold meetings in. I sure remember the
old brush arbor and the glorious times then, and
how the niggers used to sing and pray and shout. I
am a Baptist and we baptized in the creek after we
dammed it up to hold water deep enough. Sometimes, we used a waterhole in the woods. I remember one old Baptist song, it went:

> Down to the water I be baptized,
>   for my Savior die:
> Down to the water,
>   the River of Jordan,
> Where my Savior baptized.

When Freedom come, the slaves was notified that
a white man by the name Ben White would come to
the plantation and make a speech to them. He said,
"Now that you is free, you will be with your marster,
and he is willing to give you one-third of what you
make. You is free, and there will be no more whip-
pings." Then Marster said, while he was crying,
"You stay on with me, and I'll give you food and
clothes and one-third of what you make."

After the war, the Ku Klux did bad in our
neighborhood. They killed five or six niggers. I
guess it was 'cause they was Republicans and had
trouble at voting times.

I married Missouri Rice at her own house. We
had a big wedding, and she wore a white dress with
two frills on it. I wore a dove-colored suit and a
high brim hat with a small crown. I bought the hat

for seven dollars just to marry in, but used it for Sundays.

I never did think slavery was right. I was just a chap then and never thought much about it till long since it was over. I am a Democrat and always was one. I was forty years old when I repented of my sins and joined the church. I wanted to join and be baptized and be saved.

Alexander Scaife

Age 82, when interviewed by
Caldwell Sims, in Pacolet, S.C. (Box 104)

MARSTER CHARNER SCAIFE A-laying on his bed of death is about the first thing that stuck in my mind. I felt sorry for everybody then. Miss Mary Rice Scaife, his wife, was mean. She died a year after. Never felt sad nor glad then, never felt no ways out of the regular way.

Overseers I recollects was: Mr. Sam Hughes, Mr. Tom Baldwin, and Mr. Whitfield Davis. Mr. Baldwin was the best to me. He had a still-house out in a field where liquor was made. I tote it for him. We made good corn liquor. Once a week I brung a gallon to the big house to Marster. Once I got happy offen it, and when I got there, lots of it was gone. He had me whipped. That the last time I ever got happy offen Marster's jug.

When I was a shaver, I carried water to the rooms and polished shoes for all the white folks in the house. Set the freshly polished shoes at the door of the bedroom. Get a nickel for that and dance for joy over it.

Two big gals cleaned the rooms up. I helped carry out things, take up ashes, fetch wood, and build fires early every day. Marster's house had five bedrooms and a setting room. The kitchen and dining room was in the back yard. A covered passage kept them from getting wet when they went to the dining room. Marster said he had rather get cold going to eat than to have the food get cold while it was being fetched to him. So, he had the kitchen and dining room joined, but most folks had the dining room in the big house.

It took a week to take the cotton boat from Chester to Columbia. Six slaves handled the flatboat: the boatman, two oarsmen, two steermen, and an extra man. The steermen was just behind the boatman. They steered with long poles on the way up the river and paddled down the river. The two oarsmen was behind them. They used to pole, too, going up, and paddle going down.

Seventy-five or eighty bales was carried at a time. They weighed around three hundred pounds apiece. In Columbia, the wharfs was on the Congaree banks. For the cotton, we got all kinds of supplies to carry home. The boat was loaded with sugar and coffee coming back. On the Broad River, we passed by Woods Ferry, Fish Dam Ferry, Henderson's Ferry, Henderson's Island, and some others, but that is all I recollect. We unloaded at our own ferry called Scaife Ferry.

♦ ♦ ♦

Zack Herndon

Age 93, when interviewed by
Caldwell Sims, in Gaffney, S.C.,
Grenard Street; May 1937.

YES, SIR, MY OLD marster had lots of land, a big
plantation down at Lockhart where I was born,
called the Herndon Plantation. Then he live in a big
house just outside of Union, called Herndon Ter-
race, and besides that, he was the biggest lawyer
that was in Union.

First remembrance was at the age of three when
as yet I couldn't walk none. My mother cooked
some gingerbread. She told the chilluns to go down
a hill and get her some oak bark. The first one back
with the bark would get the first gingerbread cake
that was done.

My sister sat me down, a-sliding down the side of
her leg, after she had carried me with her down the
side of the hill. Them big chaps started to fooling
time away. I grab up some bark in my hand and
went toddling and a-crawling up to the house. My
mother seed me a-crawling and toddling, and she
took the bark out of my hand and let me pull up to
the door. She cook the gingerbread, and when the
other chilluns got back, I was a-setting up eating the
first cake.

She put gingerbread dough in a round oven that
had legs on it. It looked like a skillet, but it never

had no handle. It had a lid to go on the top with a groove to hold live coals. Live coals went under it, too. Mother wanted oak chips and bark, 'cause they made such good hot coals and clean ashes.

Pots boiled in the back of the chimney, a-hanging from a pot rack over the blazing fire. It had pot hooks to get it down.

Bread was cooked in a baker, like the ginger cake was. They roasted both kinds of taters in the ashes and made cornbread in the ashes and called it ash cake, then.

Us lived in a one-room log house. For the larger families, they had two rooms with the fireplace in the middle of the room. Ours was at the end by the window. It had white or red oak, or pine shingles to cover the roof with. Of course, the shingles was handmade, never knowed how to make no others.

All beds was corded. Alongside the railings, there was holes bored to draw the ropes through, as these was what they used in them days instead of slats. Ropes could be stretched to make the bed lay good. Us never had a chair in the house. My pa made benches for us to sit by the fire on. Marster Zack let the overseer get planks for us.

My pa was called Lyles Herndon. We had a large plank table that Pa made. Never had no mirrors. Went to the spring to see ourselves on a Sunday morning. Never had no such things as dressers in them days. All us had was a table, benches, and beds. And my pa made them. Had plenty wood for fire and pine knots for lights when the fire get low or stop blazing.

Us had tallow candles. Why, everybody knowed how to make tallow candles in them days, that wasn't nothing out of the ordinary. All you had to do was to kill a beef and take the tallow from his tripe and kidneys. See, it the fat you get and boil it out, stew it down just as folks does hog lard these days.

The candle moulds was made out of tin. For the wicks, all the wrapping string was saved up, and there wasn't much wrapping string in them times. Put the string right down the middle of the mould and pour the hot tallow all around it. The string will be the wick for the candle. Then the moulds was laid in real cold water so that the tallow shrink when it harden, and this allow the candle to drop easy from the mould and not break up. Why, it's just as easy to make tallow candles as it is to fall off a log.

Marster Zack had a hundred slaves on that plantation. Stout, healthy ones brung from one thousand dollars on up to two thousand dollars a head. When I was a young kid, I heard that he was offered eight hundred for me, but he never took it.

Marster Zack never bred no slaves, but us heard of such afar off. He let his darkies marry when they wanted to. He was a good man. He always allowed the slaves to marry as they pleased, 'cause he allowed that God never intent for no souls to be bred as if they was cattle. And he never practice no such.

After Mr. Herndon died, I was sold at the sale at Lockhart, to Dr. Tom Bates from Santuc. He bought me for eighteen hundred dollars, so as they always told me. This the onliest time that I was ever sold.

First lamp that I ever seed was a tin lamp. It was a little table lamp with a handle and a flat wick. That was at Dr. Bates's place in Santuc. He had it in his house. Him and his brother lived together. Dr. Bates's brother, Fair, was single man that live in the house with Dr. Bates for thirteen years. I was Dr. Bates's houseboy.

As houseboy there, I mind the flies from the table and tote dishes to and fro from the kitchen. Kitchen far ways off from the house. James Bates, his cook. Sometime I help wash the dishes. Marster never had no big house, 'cause he was late marrying. There wan't no company in them days, neither.

Rations was give out every week from the smokehouse. On Saturday, us get one peck meal, three pounds of meat, and one-half gallon black molasses for a person. That's lot more than they gets in these days and times. Sunday morning us get two, or maybe, three pounds of flour. Didn't know nothing about no fatback in them times. Had sassafras, sage teas, and dinty tea [a tea brewed from a South Carolina weed].

Twenty-five or thirty hogs was killed at the time. Lots of sheep and goats was also killed. All our meat was raised, and us wore wooden-bottom shoes. Raised all the wheat and corn. Hogs, cows, goats, and sheep just run wild on Tinker and Brushy Fork creeks.

Never seed no ice in them days 'cept in winter. Summertime, things was kept in the milk-house. Well water was changed every day to keep things cool. Everybody drink milk in the summer, and leave off hot tea, and the white folks only drink coffee for their breakfast.

Marster's saddle horse was kinder reddish. Generally, he do his practice on horseback. He good doctor, and carry his medicine in saddle bags. It was leather and fall on each side of the horse's side. When you put something in it, you have to keep it balanced. Don't never see no saddle bags, neither does you see no doctors going round on no horses, these days.

I lived in slavery for over twenty-one years. Yes,

I's twenty-one when Freedom come. Then Dr. Bates up and marry Mr. Henry Sartor's daughter, Miss Mary. Don't know how long she live, but she up and took and died. Then he pop up and marry her sister, Anne. It was already done Freedom when he marry the first time. When he married the second time, Mr. Fair up and went over to the Keenan place to live. He never did marry, hisself, though.

My son took me back to Union last year, 1936. Nothing didn't look natural, 'cept the jail. Everything else look strange. Didn't see nobody I knowed, not nary living soul. Marster's big white house, with them columns, still setting there, but the front all growed up in pine trees. When I slave-time darky, that front had flowers and figures setting all along the drive from the road to the big house. Tain't like that now.

◆ ◆ ◆

Adeline Johnson

Age 93, when interviewed by
W. W. Dixon in Winnsboro, S.C.

I BORN ON WHAT is now called the Jesse Gladden place, but it all belong to my old marster, William Hall, then.

My old marster was one of the richest men in the world. Him have lands in Chester and Fairfield counties, Georgia and Florida, and one place on the Red River in Arkansas. He also had a plantation to raise brown sugar on, in old Louisiana. Then him and his brother Daniel built and give Bethesda Church, that's standing yet, to the white Methodists of Mitford, for them to attend and worship at. He remembered the Lord, you see, in all his ways and the Lord guide his steps.

I never have to do no field work, just stayed round the house and wait on the missus, and the chillun. I was whipped just one time. That was for marking the mantelpiece with a dead coal of fire. They make Mammy do the lashing. Hadn't hit me three licks before Miss Dorcas, Miss Jemima, Miss Julia, and Marster Johnnie run there, catch the switch, and say, "That enough, Mama Ann! Addie won't do it again." That's all the beating I ever received in slavery time.

I was about raised up in the house. In the evening, I fill them boxes with chips and fat splinters. When morning come, I go in there and make a fire for my young missuses to get up by. I help dress them and comb their hair. Then, I goes downstairs and put flowers on the breakfast table and lay the Bible by Marster William's chair. Then I bring in the breakfast. Table have to be set the night before. When everything was on the table, I ring the bell. White folks come down, and I wait on the table.

After the meal finish, Marster William read the Bible and pray. I clear the table and help wash the dishes. When that finish, I cleans up the rooms. Then, I acts as maid and waitress at dinner and supper. I warms up the girls' room, where they sleep, after supper. Then go home to Poppy John and Mama Ann. That was a happy time, with happy days.

The white folks near was the Mellichamps, the Gladdens, the Mobleys, Lumpkins, Boulwares, Fords, Picketts, and Johnsons.

After Freedom I marry a preacher, Tom Johnson. Him die when in his sixties, thirty years ago. I hope and prays to get to heaven. I'll be satisfied to see my Savior that my old marster worshipped and my husband preach about. I want to be in heaven with all my white folks, just to wait on them, and love them, and serve them, sorta like I did in slavery time. That will be enough heaven for Adeline.

Rebecca Jane Grant

Age 92, when interviewed by
Phoebe Faucette, in Lena, S.C.

I WAS JUST A little girl, about eight years old, staying in Beaufort at the missus' house, polishing her brass andirons and scrubbing her floors, when one morning she say to me, "Janie, take this note down to Mr. Wilcox Wholesale Store on Bay Street and fetch me back the package the clerk give you."

I took the note. The man read it, and he say, "Uh-huh." Then he turn away and he come back with a little package, which I took back to the missus.

She open it when I bring it in and say, "Go upstairs, Miss!"

It was a raw cowhide strap about two feet long, and she started to pouring it on me all the way upstairs. I didn't know what she was whipping me about, but she pour it on, and she pour it on.

Directly, she say, "You can't say 'Marster Henry,' Miss? You can't say 'Marster Henry?' "

"Yes'm. Yes'm. I can say 'Marster Henry!' "

Marster Henry was just a little boy about three or four years old. Come about halfway up to me. Wanted me to say "Marster" to him—a baby!

My mother and four of us children were sold to Mr. Robert Oswald in Beaufort. My father belong

138

to Marster Tom Willingham, but my mother belong to another white man. Marster Tom was always trying to buy us so we could all be together, but the man wouldn't sell us to him. We had to leave all the folks we know when we was took to Beaufort.

All of us chillun, too little to work, used to have to stay at the "Street" [slave quarters]. They'd have some old folks to look after us—some old man or some old woman. They'd clean off a place on the ground near the washpot where they cooked the peas, clean it off real clean, then pile the peas out there on the ground for us to eat. We'd pick 'em up in our hands and begin to eat.

Sometimes, they'd cook hoecakes in a fire of coals. They'd mix a little water with the meal and make a stiff dough that could be patted into shape with the hands. The cakes would be put right into the fire and would be washed off clean after they were raked out from the coals.

My mother say she didn't know a soul. All the time she'd be praying to the Lord. She'd take us chillun to the woods to pick up firewood, and we'd turn around to see her down on her knees behind a stump, a-praying. We'd see her wiping her eyes with the corner of her apron, first one eye, then the other, as we come along back. Then, back in the house, down on her knees, she'd be a-praying. One night she say she been down on her knees a-praying and that when she got up, she looked out the door and there she saw coming down out the elements a man, pure white and shining.

He got right before her door, and come and stand right to her feet, and say, "Sarah, Sarah, Sarah. You're not parted from your husband. You're just over a little slash of water. Who do you put your trust in?"

My mother say, after that, everything just flow along, just as easy. Now my mother was an unusually good washer and ironer. The white folks had been saying, "Wonder who it is that's making the clothes look so good?" Well, about this time, they found out; and they would come bringing her plenty of washing to do. And when they would come, they would bring her a pan full of food for us chilluns.

Soon the other white folks from round about heard of her, and she was getting all the washing she needed. She would wash for the missus during the day, and for the other folks at night. And they all was good to her.

One day the missus call her to the house to read her something from a letter she got. The letter say that my father had married another woman. My mother was so upset she say, "I hope he breaks that woman's jawbone. She know she ain't his lawful wife." And they say her wish come true. That was just what happened.

They used to make the clothes for the slaves in the house. Had a seamstress to stay there in the house so the missus could supervise the work. The cloth the clothes was made out of was handwoven. It was dyed in pretty colors—some green, some blue, and pretty colors. And it was strong cloth, too. Times got so hard during the war that the white folks had to use the cloth woven by hand, themselves.

The ladies would wear bustles, and hoops made out of oak. Old times, they'd make underbodies with whalebone in it. There was something they'd put over the hoop they call "follow me, boy." Used to wear the skirts long, with them long trains that trail behind you. You'd take and tuck it up behind on some little hook or something they had to fasten it up to. And the little babes had long dresses. Come down to your feet when you hold the baby in your lap. And embroidered from the bottom of the skirt all the way up. Oh, they were embroidered up in the finest sort of embroidery.

Didn't have no colored churches. The drivers and the overseers, the house-servants, the bricklayers, and folks like that'd go to the white folks' church. But not the field hands. Why, they couldn't have all got in the church. My marster had three or four hundred slaves, himself. And most of the other white folks had just as many or more. But them as went would *sing*. Oh, they'd sing! I remember two of them specially. One was a man and he'd sing bass. Oh, he'd roll it down! The other was a woman, and she'd sing soprano. They had colored preachers to preach to the field hands down in the quarters. They'd preach in the street. Meet next day to the marster's and turn in the report. How many pray, how many ready for baptism, and all like that.

Used to have Sabbath school in the white people's house, on the porch, on Sunday evening. The porch was big and they'd fill that porch. They never fail to give the chillun Sabbath school. Learn them the Sabbath catechism. And they was taught they must be faithful to the missus and marster's work like you would to your heavenly Father's work.

We'd sing a song the church bells used to ring in Beaufort. You never hear it anymore. But I remembers it:

> I want to be an angel, and with an
>   angel stand,
> A crown upon my forehead, a harp
>   within my hand.

Right there before my Savior, so
   glorious and so bright,
I'll hear the sweetest music, and
   praise Him day and night.

At the white folks' church at Lawtonville, they had a colored man who used to sing for them by the name of Moses Murray. He'd sit there back of the organ and roll down on them bass. Roll down just like the organ roll! He was Moses Lawton at that time, you know.

I was fifteen years old when I left Beaufort, at the time Freedom was declared. We were all re-united then. First, my mother and the young chillun, then I got back. My uncle, Jose Jenkins, come to Beaufort and stole me by night from my missus. He took me with him to his home in Savannah. We had been done freed, but he stole me away from the house.

When my father heard that I wasn't with the others, he sent my grandfather, Isaac, to hunt me. When he find me at my uncle's house, he took me back. We walked back—all sixty-four miles. I was foundered. You know, if a foundered person will jump over a stick of burning lightwood, it will make 'em feel better.

You know how old I am? I'm in my ninety-fourth year. Ella has a dream book she looks up my age in and tells me what luck I have, and all that. I generally had good luck.

♦ ♦ ♦

Elijah Green

*Age 94, when interviewed by
Augustus Ladson, at 156 Elizabeth Street,
Charleston, S.C.*

FROM THE SOUTHEAST OF Calhoun Street, which was then Boundary Street, to the Battery was the city limit. And from the northwest of Boundary Street for several miles was nothing but farm land. All my brothers was farm hands for our marster, George W. Jones. I was born in Charleston at 82 King Street, December 25, 1843. The house is still there who recent owner is Judge Whaley. My ma and pa was Kate and John Green.

I did all the housework till the war, when I was given to Mr. George W. Jones's son, William, as his "daily give" [a valet] servant who duty was to clean his boots, shoes, sword, and make his coffee. He was First Lieutenant of the South Carolina Company Regiment.

Being his servant, I wear all his cast-off clothes, which I was glad to have. My shoes was called brogan, that had brass on the toe. When a slave had one of them, you couldn't tell them he wasn't dressed to death.

As the daily give servant of Mr. William H. Jones, I had to go to Virginia during the war. In the battle at Richmond, General Lee had General Grant almost beaten. When General Sherman got to Virginia, the battle was renewed and continued for seven days, at the end of which General Lee surrender to General Grant.

During the seven days' fight, the battle got so hot till Mr. William Jones made his escape, and it was two days before I know he was gone. One of the generals sent me home, and I got here two days before Mr. William got home. He went up in the attic and stay there till the war was end. I carry all his meals to him and tell him all the news. Marster sure was a frightened man; I was sorry for him. That battle at Richmond, Virginia, was the worst in American history.

Mr. Ryan had a private Jail on Queen Street near the Planters' Hotel. He was very cruel; he'd lick his slaves to death. Very seldom one of his slaves survive a whipping. He was the opposite to Governor Aiken, who live on the northwest corner of Elizabeth and Judith streets. He had several rice plantations, hundreds of his slaves he didn't know.

Not till John C. Calhoun's body was carried down Boundary Street was the name changed in his honor. He is buried in St. Phillip's Churchyard, across the street, with a laurel tree planted at his head. Four men and me dig his grave, and I cleared the spot where his monument now stand. The monument was put up by Pat Collington, a Charleston mason. I never did like Calhoun, 'cause he hated the Negro. No man was ever hated as much as him by a group of people.

The Work House (Sugar House) was on Magazine Street, built by Mr. Columbus G. Trumbone. On Charlmer [Chalmers] Street is the slave market from which slaves was taken to Vangue Range and auctioned off. At the foot of Lawrence Street, opposite East Bay Street, on the other side of the trolley tracks is where Mr. Alonzo White kept and sell slaves from his kitchen. He was a slave broker who had a house that extended almost to the train tracks, which is about three hundred yards going to the waterfront. No train or trolley tracks was there then, cause there was only one railroad here, the Southern, and the depot was on Ann Street, where the Bagging Mill now is.

When slaves run away and their marsters catch them, to the stockade they go, where they'd be whipped every other week for a number of months. And for God's sake, don't let a slave be catch with pencil and paper. That was a major crime. You might as well had killed your marster or missus.

One song I know I used to sing to the slaves when marster went away, but I wouldn't be so fool as to let him hear me. What I can remember of it is:

> Marster gone away,
> But darkies stay at home,
> The year of Jubilee is come,
> And Freedom will begun.

The first two people that was hung in Charleston was Harry and Janie, husband and wife who was slaves of Mr. Christopher Black. Mr. Black had them whipped and they planned to kill the whole family. They poisoned the breakfast one morning, and if two of the family hadn't oversleep, they too would a-been dead. The others die almost instantly. An investigation was made and the poison discovered, and the two slaves hung on the big oak tree in the middle of Ashley Avenue.

When any in your owner's family was going to be married, the slaves was dressed in linen clothes to witness the ceremony. Only special slaves was chosen to be at the wedding. Slaves was always asked how they like the one who was coming in the family. I didn't like that, 'cause I had to lie on myself by saying nice things about the person and hate the person at the same time.

Slaves was always buried in the night, as no one could stop to do it in the day. Old boards was used to make the coffin that was blackened with shoe polish.

Mr. Stiles Bee, on James Island, give tract of land to the Negroes for a school just after the war. He put up a shed-like building with a few chairs in it. It was at the place called Cut Bridge.

After the war I did garden work. I was janitor at Benedict College in Columbia for two years and at Claflin in Orangeburg for twelve. Now all that is past, and I'm living from hand to mouth. The banks took all my money and I can't work or do the collecting for my landlord, and he give me a room free. If it wasn't for that, I don't know what I'd do.

◆ ◆ ◆

Amy Perry

Age 82, when interviewed by
Jessie A. Butler, at 21 Pitt Street,
Charleston, S.C.; May 1937.

WE IS LIVE IN the country, near Orangeburg, and I remembers very little about the war and the time before the war. The colored people make they own cloth and call 'em cotton osnaburg. They make banyans for the chillun. Sleeve been cut in the cloth, and they draw it up at the neck, and call 'em banyan [from the body garment worn by *banians,* or Indian traders, in West Africa]. They ain't know nothing about drawers nor nothing like that.

The medicine I remember was castor oil, and dogwood and cherry bark, which they put in whiskey and give you. They is give you this to keep your blood good. Dogwood will bitter your blood; it good medicine, I know.

I remember the people have to get ticket for go out at night. When they is gone to prayer meeting, I is see them drag bush back of them, to outen they step [obliterate footprints]. If the patrol catch you without ticket, they beat you.

I remembers when the Yankee come through and Wheeler army come after us. Those been dreadful times. The Yankees massacred the people, burned their houses, and stole the meat and everything they could find. The white folks have to live wher-

147

ever they can, and they didn't have enough to eat. I know whole families live on one goose a week, cooked in greens. Sometimes they have punkin and corn, red corn at that. Times was hard, hard. The colored people didn't have nothing to eat neither. That why my aunty bring me to Charleston to live.

The first year after Freedom, I gone to school on Mr. John Townsend place, down to Rockville. After peace declared, the colored people lived on cornmeal mush and salt water in the week, and mush and vinegar for Sunday. Mind you, that for Sunday! I don't see how we live, yet we is.

About eight year after the war, we used to go down to the dairy for clabber. They give you so much for each one in the family—two tablespoon full for the grown people and one tablespoon for the chilluns. We add water to that and make a meal. In the country, the colored people live on a third [one-third of the season's crop], but, of course, at the end of the year, they didn't have nothing. Yet, they has lived.

Some people believe in dreams, but I don't have no faith in them. Lot of people believe in root and such, but they can't scare me with root. I roll over them from here to Jericho and they wouldn't bother me. A man died bad right in that house yonder. I went with the doctor, close his sight, and such; and I come right home, gone to bed, and sleep. He ain't bother me and I ain't see him since. I don't believe in ghosts, nor dreams, nor conjure, that the worst.

Some people say they can see ghost, but you can't see ghost and live. I don't believe in 'um, no ghost, and no conjure, though my Uncle Cotton Judson and my Aunt Massie both believe in them. Uncle Cotton could do most as much as the devil he-self; he could most fly, but I never believe in 'um, no matter what he can do.

As long as old people live, they going to tell the young ones about ghost and thing. They going to pass it on. And when they die, they going to leave that foolishness right here. No, I don't believe in no conjure and no root. If they give me poison, then they got me.

You can eat your stomach full, and you'll dream. I believe in some kind of vision. You doze off, and you have a good dream. I believe that. People get converted in dreams. I was twelve year old when I get converted. I dreamed I was in a field, a large green field. A girl was there that I didn't had no use for. I had a bundle on my back. I honey the girl up and love 'um and the bundle fall on the ground. They put me in the church then.

◆ ◆ ◆

Willis Williams

Age 89/90, when interviewed by
Genevieve W. Chandler,
in Conway, S.C.; May 1935.

WHEN I WAS BORN, been August. I was a man
grown pulling boxes [turpentine boxes] when
the shake was [the 1886 earthquake]. I know the
very night the shake come—on a Wednesday night.
I was on doorstep, loosing my shoestring. There was
more religion then than they is now. Praying and
prayer meeting for a month. Everybody tend meeting.

The man I belonged to been Marster John A.
Williams, born on the Cape Fear. I goes by Marster
John name—Williams.

Marster John Williams had four hundred slaves.
He was a man *had* the colored people. He didn't
work all on his own plantation. He'd hire out his
people to work turpentine—put 'em out for so much
a year. He'd give 'em blanket, suit, coat, pants.
First of the year come, Boss would collect wages for
all he hire out.

When I was houseboy for old Marster John, wait-
ing on white people, that was the best and easiest
time I ever had. Ever Saturday, drive Marster John
to Fayetteville. Ever Saturday, they'd think that
store belong to me. I'd eat lumps of brown sugar
out the barrel, candy, crackers. Did as I please
then, now do as I can.

Remember when the Yankees come. Been Sunday morning. Ride up to the gate on horses. Old Boss happened to come out and walk to the lot. I happened to be at gate. They took his watch out his pocket, his pistol—had it girded to him—and took all he whiskey and catch chickens and guinea and take them all. Then, they gone in the lot and took two breeding mares and hitch them in wagon and loaded wagon full of corn. Then, they took the two carriage horses and hitched to carriage, gone to smokehouse, and fill that carriage full of all Marster John sides of meat and ham and shoulders.

I been following and watching to see what all they going to take, and a soldier looked at me and say, "come on, little nigger! Wanter go?"

And I done like another fool. I rode off behind the two brood mares, on the corn, and where they rested that night, I rested right there.

It was mighty cold up there. I suffered a heap in the cold before I got back home. They give me a horse—saddled and bridled—and a little bayonet gun. Put me on that horse to drive cattle. Tell me to take all I see. Didn't except *nobody* cattle. Night come, put 'em in pasture—put 'em in *anybody* field—on the oats, rye, wheat.

Sometimes, rain sure fall. Had to tend that bunch of cattle, rain or no rain. Didn't kill one beef and stop. *Four* beeves a day. Go out, get the hog, and kill 'em. Skin 'em. Didn't scald 'em and clean 'em like we do. Just eat the ham. Rest throw away. Gone to Wilmington, Fayetteville, Rockfish, and Beaver Creek.

General Sherman? I *seen* him. He had a big name, but he warn't such a big man. He was a little spare-made man. I remember now when I seed him the last time. He had two matched horses going down to Petersburg. Six guards riding by the side of his turnout. Oh my God, what clothes he had on! He was dressed down in finest uniform.

I remember it was Sunday morning that General Johnson throwed up his hand at Raleigh. Done with the war.

When I leave the Yankee, they give me thirty-five dollars in money. I been so fool, had never seen no greenback. Throwed it away eating crackers and peanuts. And I bought some brogan shoes. If I'd a helt on to that, I'd a-been somebody today.

Before Freedom, I have a good enough time. Just lay round the house and wait on my boss. When Freedom come and I did have to get out and work, it most kill me.

After Freedom, my mother wash for family to Beaver Creek. And after Freedom, my father went to working on shares. Old Marster John called 'em up and tell 'em, "You free, Asa. You free, Lewis. You free, Handy. You free, Wash. You can do as you please. You have to fadge for yourself now."

That there my second wife. How many wife I had? Two or three. Lemme see—[looking at present wife], you is one. You the last one. First one been Jinny Lind. Next one been Mary Dickson. And Caressa Pyatt been one. And there been another one. I forgot that woman name. Got it in my mouth and can't call it. I'll call the name of them others I take up with in a little while. One was Caroline; one was Tisha. I take them a little while; and if they didn't do to suit me, I put 'em out. Some I didn't stay with long enough to find out they name. Jinny Lind sister was Tisha. Jinny Lind gone, try her sister. Just a make-out. If they didn't do to suit me, I'd give 'em the devil and put 'em out.

Woman, dog, cypress knee,
More you beat em, the better they be!

But some woman, the more you beat 'em, the
worse the devil gets in 'em. Get so they won't "gee"
nor "haw." "Ways of woman and ways of snake
deeper than the sea." I take that to mean mighty
few can tell by the trail of a snake whether it's
coming or going.

I hear story about the rabbit and the fox—all
them old things—some times my mind franzy [fuzzy].
Been break up too much. Break two ribs to the
lumber mill. Jump out a cart one day and run a
ten-penny nail through my foot. That lay me up two
months. Some mean people catch me up by that
tree yonder with a car, and that lay me up sixty-five
days. They pick me up for dead that time. All that
make my mind get franzy sometimes. Come and go.
Come and go.

♦ ♦ ♦

Sam Polite

Age 93, when interviewed by
Chlotilde R. Martin, in Beaufort County, S.C.

WHEN GUN SHOOT ON Bay Point for Freedom, I been seventeen-year-old working slave. I born on B. Fripp Plantation, on St. Helena Island. My father belong to Mr. Marion Fripp, and my mother belong to Mr. Old B. Fripp. I don't know how mucher land, neither how much slave he have, but he have two big plantation and many slave—more'n a hundred slave.

Slave live on street—two row of house with two room to the house. My father and mother ain't marry. Slave don't marry; they just live together. All slave have for stay on plantation in daytime, but when work done, can visit wife on other plantation. Have pass, so patrol won't get 'um.

When I been little boy, I play on street—shoot marble, play army, and such thing. When horn blow and morning star rise, slave have for get up and cook. When day clean [after sunrise], they gone to field. Woman too old for work in field have for stay on street and mind baby. Old mens follow cow. Chillun don't work in field till twelve or thirteen year old. You carry dinner to field in your can and leave 'um at the heading [top of row]. When you feel hungry, you eat.

Every slave have task [quarter acre] to do, some-time one task, sometime two task, and sometime three. You have for work till task through. When cotton done make, you have other task. Have to cut cord of marsh grass maybe. Task of marsh been eight feet long and four feet high. Then, sometime you have to roll cord of mud in cowpen. Woman have to rake leaf from wood into cowpen.

When you knock off work, you can work on your land. Maybe you might have two or three task of land round your cabin what Marster give you for plant. You can have chicken, maybe hog. You can sell egg and chicken to store and Marster will buy your hog. In that way, slave can have money for buy thing like fish and whatever he want. We don't get much fish in slavery, 'cause we never have boat. But sometime you can throw out net and catch shrimp. You can also catch possum and raccoon with your dog.

On Saturday night, every slave that works gets peck of corn and pea, and sometime meat and clabber. You never see any sugar, neither coffee, in slavery. You has straw in your mattress, but they give you blanket. Every year, in Christmas month, you gets four or either five yard cloth, according to how you is. Out of that, you have to make your clote [clothes]. You wears that same clote till the next year. You wear it winter and summer, Sunday and every day. You don't get no coat, but they give you shoe.

In slavery, you don't know nothing about sheets for your bed. Us never know nothing about Santa Claus till Freedom, but on Christmas, Marster give you meat and syrup and maybe three day without work.

Slave work till dark on Saturday just like any

other day. I still does work till dark on Saturday. But on Sunday, slave don't work. On Fourth of July, slave work till twelve o'clock and then knocks off. On Sunday, slave can visit back and forth on the plantations.

Slave don't do mucher frolic. When woman have baby, he [Gullah speech often substitutes masculine for other pronouns, including possessives] have mid-wife for nine day and sometime don't have to work for month when baby born. Missus send clote from Big House. When nigger sick, Marster send doctor. If you been very sick, doctor give you calomus or castor oil. Sometime he give you Dead-Shot for worms, or Puke [a powder] to make you heave. If I just have a pain in my stomach, my mother give me Juse-e-moke [Jerusalem artichoke], what he get out of the wood.

If slave don't do task, they get licking with lash on naked back. Driver nigger give licking, but Marster most always been there. Sometime maybe nigger steal hog or run away to the wood, then he get licking, too. Can't be no trouble between white folks and nigger in slavery time, for they do as they choose with you. But Marster good to slave, if they done they's task and don't be up to no meanness. Missus don't have nothing to do with nigger.

In slavery, nigger go to white folks' church. Slave don't know nothing about baptizing. When nigger dead, you can't knock off work for bury 'um. You have to wait till nighttime to put 'um in the grave. You bury 'um by the light of torch. Old Man Tony Ford been the man what attend to funerals. They wasn't no nigger preacher on the plantation, but they been people to hold prayers.

I never see nigger in chain, but I see them in stock. I see plenty nigger sell on banjo [makeshift;

sawhorse] table. They put you up on platform and they buy you. I see my uncle sell; he brung one hundred dollar. Woman don't sell without her chillun.

Mr. Johnnie Fripp been my young marster. When he chillun get marry, Old Marster divide the nigger. He give Marster Johnnie thirty slave, and I been one of them. Marster buy plantation on the Main [mainland]. He build big house. He have four boy and two gal. He have five hundred acre. He ain't have no overseer, just driver. We don't know no poor white trash on the Main, neither on St. Helena Island.

I work in field on Marster Johnnie Fripp plantation. Sometime we sing when us work. One song we sing been go like this:

> Go way, Old Man
> Go way, Old Man;
> Where you been all day?
> If you treat me good,
> I'll stay till the Judgment Day.
> But if you treat me bad,
> I'll sure to run away.

When war come, Missus take me and two more niggers, put we and chillun in two wagon, and go to Barnwell. My mother been one of the nigger. We stay in Barnwell all during the war. My father, he been with the Rebel, been with Mr. Marion Chaplin. When Freedom come, Missus didn't say nothing; she just cry. But she give we a wagon and we press [stole] a horse and us come back to St. Helena Island. It take three day to get home.

When we get home, we find the rest of the nigger here been have Freedom four year before we.

I work for a nigger name Peter White. My father

come back and buy twenty acre of land, and we all live together. I gone to school one or two year, but I ain't learn much. Four year after war, I buy fifteen acre of land. That was this here same place where I lives now. After while I goes to work in rock [phosphate mines]. I hears about Ku Klux. They been bad people. They will kill you.

Been marry to four wife. This here last one, he been born in slavery too, but he don't remembers much about 'um. He been little gal so high, just big enough for open gate for white folks.

Fannie Griffin

Age 94, when interviewed by
Everett R. Pierce,
2125 Calhoun Street, Columbia S.C.

MY MARSTER, MARSTER JOE Beard, was a good man, but he wasn't one of the richest men. He only had six slaves, three men and three women. But he had a big plantation and would borrow slaves from his brother-in-law, on the adjoining plantation, to help with the crops.

I was the youngest slave, so Missy Grace, that's Marster Joe's wife, keep me in the house most of the time, to cook and keep the house cleaned up. I milked the cow and worked in the garden, too.

My marster was good to all he slaves, but Missy Grace was mean to us. She whip us a heap of times when we ain't done nothing bad to be whipped for. When she go to whip me, she tie my wrists together with a rope and put that rope through a big staple in the ceiling and draw me up off the floor and give me a hundred lashes. I think about my old mammy heap of times now and how I's seen her whipped, with the blood dripping off of her.

All that us slaves know how to do was to work hard. We never learn to read and write. Nor we never had no church to go to, only sometimes the white folks let us go to their church, but we never join in the singing. We just set and listen to them preach and pray.

The graveyard was right by the church and heap of the colored people was scared to go by it at night. They say they see ghosts and hants and spirits, but I ain't never see none, don't believe there is none. I more scared of live people than I is dead ones; dead people ain't going to harm you.

Our marster and missus was good to us when we was sick. They send for the doctor right off and the doctor do all he could for us, but he ain't had no kind of medicine to give us 'cepting spirits of turpentine, castor oil, and a little blue mass. They ain't had all kinds of pills and stuff then, like they has now. But I believe we ain't been sick as much then as we do now. I never heard of no consumption them days; us had pneumonia sometimes, though.

We never was allowed to have no parties nor dances, only from Christmas Day to New Year's Eve. We had plenty good things to eat on Christmas Day and Santa Claus was good to us, too. We'd have all kinds of frolics from Christmas to New Year's, but never was allowed to have no fun after that time.

I remembers one time I slip off from the missus and go to a dance, and when I come back, the dog in the yard didn't seem to know me and he bark and wake the missus up, and she whip me something awful. I sure didn't go to no more dances without asking her.

The patrollers would catch you, too, if you went out after dark. We most times stay at home at night and spin cloth to make our clothes. We make all our clothes, and our shoes was handmade, too. We didn't have fancy clothes like the people has now. I likes it better being a slave. We got along better then, than we do now. We didn't have to pay for everything we had.

The worst time we ever had was when the Yankee men come through. We heard they was coming, and the missus tell us to put on a big pot of peas to cook. So we put some white peas in a big pot and put a whole ham in it, so that we'd have plenty for the Yankees to eat. Then, when they come, they kicked the pot over and the peas went one way and the ham another.

The Yankees destroyed most everything we had. They come in the house and told the missus to give them her money and jewels. She started crying and told them she ain't got no money or jewels, 'cepting the ring she had on her finger. They got awfully mad and started destroying everything. They took the cows and horses, burned the gin, the barn, and all the houses 'cept the one Marster and Missus was living in.

They didn't leave us a thing 'cept some big hominy and two banks of sweet potatoes. We chipped up some sweet potatoes and dried them in the sun, then we parched them and ground them up and that's all we had to use for coffee. It taste pretty good, too. For a good while, we just live on hominy and coffee.

We ain't had no celebration after we was freed. We ain't know we was free till a good while after. We ain't know it till General Wheeler come through and tell us. After that, the marster and missus let all the slaves go 'cepting me; they kept me to work in the house and the garden.

Silvia Chisolm

Age 88, when interviewed by
Phoebe Faucette, in Estill, S.C., RFD

I BEEN EIGHT YEAR old when they took me. Took me from me mother and father here on the Pipe Creek place down to Black Swamp. Went down forty-two mile to the overseer. Mr. Beestinger was his name. And his wife, Miss Carrie. I was minding the overseer's chillun. Old man Joe Bostick was me marster. And I knows the missus and the marster used to work us. Had the overseer to drive us. Mr. Bostick was a good old man. He been deaf. His chillun tend to his business—his sons. He was a preacher. His father was old man Ben Bostick.

I never see my mother or my father anymore. Not till after Freedom. And when I come back then I been married. But when I move back here, I stay right on this Pipe Creek place from then on. I been right here all the time.

The Pipe Creek Church was Old Missus Bostick's mammy's church. When the big church burn down by the Yankees, they give the place to the colored folks. Stephen Drayton was the first pastor the colored folks had. They named the church Canaan Baptist Church. Start from a bush arbor. The white folks' church was painted white, inside and out. It was ceiled inside.

This church didn't have no gallery for the colored folks. Didn't make no graveyard at Pipe Creek. Bury at Black Swamp. And at Lawtonville. The people leave that church and go to Lawtonville to worship. They been worshipping at Lawtonville ever since before I could wake up to know. The Pipe Creek Church just stood there, with no service in it, till the Yankee burn it. The church at Lawtonville been a fine church. Didn't burn it. Use it for a hospital during the war.

I been fifteen year old when the Yankee come— fifteen the sixth of June. I saw 'em burn down me marster's home, and everything. I remembers that. Work us till the Yankees come. When Yankee come, they had to run. That how the building burn. After they didn't find no one in it, they burn. The Marshall house had a poor white women in it. That why it didn't burn. My marster's Pineland place at Garnett was burn, too. They never did build this one back. After they come back, they build their house at the Pineland place.

After I work for Mr. Beestinger, I wait on Mr. Blunt. You know Mr. Blunt, ain't you? His place out there now.

I's eighty-eight year old now and can't remember so much. And I's blind. Blind in both eye.

Prince Smith

*Age 100+, when interviewed by
Augustus Ladson, on Wardmalaw Island, S.C.*

I WAS BORN AND raised on this island and was only from here when the Civil War had begun. When Fort Sumter was fired on, Marster carried seventy of us to Greenville, South Carolina, on account of its mountainous sections, which was believed would have prevented the Yankee invasion in regard to their hideout. We stayed in Greenville nearly four years. During that time, Marster planted his farm and we work as if we was right here.

The Yankees had gunboats, but they didn't help them at all. They couldn't make any attack that this place is so unsuited for water battles. But forest battles was fight on Beaufort Island and Port Royal. We in Greenville didn't know anything about what was going on, except what was brought to us colored people by those who was sent to the town. Marster didn't tell us anything.

For almost four years we stayed in Greenville, when suddenly one Tuesday morning bright and early, Sheridan came into Greenville on horsebacks and order everybody to surrender. Colonels and generals come in the city without the firing of a gun. We stayed there till harvesting time by the

orders of Marster Deland Bailey, who saw to it that
we was given money as a share for our work.

Marster's custom at the end of the week was to
give a dry peck of corn, which you had to grind on
Saturday evening when his work was done. Only on
Christmas, he killed and give a piece of meat. The
driver did the distribution of the ration. All young
men was given four quarts of corn a week, while the
grown men was given six quarts. All of us could
plant as much land as we would for our own use.
We could raise fowls. My marster was a gentleman;
he treat all his slaves good. My father and me was
his favorite.

Some of the slaves had to work on Sunday to
finish their week's work. If they didn't, the driver,
who was a Negro, would give a lashing varying from
fifteen to twenty-five chops. Only high-class marsters
had Negro drivers; the crackers had white overseers.

Like other slaves had to hide from their marsters
to have meeting, we could have ours any night we
want to, even without his consent. When Marster
went to town, any of his slaves could ask him to buy
things for them in Charleston. When Jews and ped-
dlers come with clothes and gunger [trinkets] to sell,
we as chillun would go to him and ask for money to
buy what we want.

He had about four hundred acres of land, which
he divided in two half by a fence. One year he
would plant one and let the cattles pasture on the
other. We could also raise hogs along with his, but
had to change pasture when he did. The people on
his plantation didn't have any need to steal from
him, for he didn't allow us to want for anything.

There was three kinds of day's work on the plantation. One is the whole task, meaning a whole hand,
or a person in his prime. He was given two task for

his day's work. A task carried from twenty-four to twenty-five rows, which was thirty-five feet long and twenty-five feet wide. The three-fourth hand was given one whole task, which consists of twelve rows. All the young chillun was included in this group. Us half-hand was the old slaves who did a half task for their day's work.

When it was time to pick cotton, the three-fourth hand had to pick thirty pound and the half-hand twenty for their day's work. Those who attended to the gin only include the three-fourth hand.

Marster had three kinds of punishment for those who disobeyed him. One was the sweat box. That was made the height of the person and no larger. Just large enough so the person didn't have to be squeezed in. The box is nailed, and in summer is put in the hot sun; in winter it is put in the coldest, dampest place. The next is the stock. Wood is nailed on or with the person lying on his back with hands and feet tied with a heavy weight on chest. The third is the Bilbao [or bilbo: foot shackles]. You are place on a high scaffold for so many hours, and you don't try to keep a level head, you'll fall and you will surely hurt yourself, if your neck isn't broken. Most of the time they were put there so they could break their necks.

George Briggs

Age 88, when interviewed by
Caldwell Sims, at RFD 2, Union, S.C.;
June 1937.

GIVE MY NAME RIGHT flat, it's George Briggs.
Give it round, it like this, George McDuffie
Briggs. My papa's name was Ike Wilburn, and my
mother's name was Margaret Briggs. Pa belonged
to Marster Lige Wilburn. Mama belonged to Jesse
(Black Jesse) Briggs. They both born and raised in
Union County.

I was born on Gist Briggs's plantation in Union
County, in the lower section of Cross Keys. My
marster was called "Black Jesse," but the reason
for that was to keep him from getting mixed up with
the other Jesse. He was the blacksmith for all the
Cross Keys section, and for that very thing he got
the name by everybody. "Black Jesse." I always
belonged to that man and he was the kindest man
what the countryside had knowledge of.

Marster and Missus was good to us all. Missus'
name was Nancy. She die early and her grave is in
Cross Keys at the Briggs graveyard. Be still! Let me
get my mind together so that I don't get mixed up
and can get you the Briggses together. Here 'tis:
Cheney and Lucindy. Lucindy married a Floyd from
Spartanburg, and the Floyds lived at the Burnt Factory. Cheney Briggs had a son Henry Briggs.

Not so fast for I'm going to start way back, that time when us was little darky boys way back in slavery. When us was real little, we played horse. Before Cheney Briggs went to Arkansas, he was our play horse. His brother Henry was the wagoner and I was the mule. Henry was little and he rid our backs sometimes. Henry rid Old Man Sam, sometimes, and Old Man Sam just holler and haw-haw at us chilluns. This was in such early childhood that is not so I can exactly map out the exact age us was then. Anyway, from this we rid the gentle horses and mules and learnt how to feed them. We started to work with the marster's mules and horses.

In that day we lived in a log cabin or house. Sometimes us never had nothing to do. Our house had only one room, but some of the houses had two rooms. Ours had a window, a door, and a common fireplace. Now they makes a fireplace to scare the wood away. In old days, they made fireplaces to take care of the chilluns in the cold weather. It warm the whole house, 'cause it was so big and there was plenty wood. Wood wasn't no problem then, and it ain't no problem yet out in the lower Keys.

When I was a little shaver and come to myself, I was sleeping in a corded bed. I just studying for a minute, can't exactly identify my grandpa, but I can identify my grandma. We all raised on the same place together. I was raised strict.

When I got big and couldn't play 'round at chillun's doings, I started to plaiting corn shucks and things for making horse and mule collars, and scouring brooms and shoulder-mats. I cut hickory poles and make handles out of them for the brooms. Marster had hides tanned and us make buggy whips, wagon whips, shoestrings, saddle strings, and such as that out of our home-tanned leather. All the galluses that was wore in them days was made by the darkies.

White oak and hickory was split to cure, and we made fish baskets, feed baskets, wood baskets, sewing baskets, and all kinds of baskets for the missus. All the chair bottoms of straight chairs was made from white oak splits, and the straight chairs was made in the shop.

You make a scouring brush like this: by splitting a width of narrow splits (keep on till you lay a entire layer of splits), turn this way, then that way, and then bind together and that hold them like you want them to stay. Last, you work in a pole as long as you want it for the handle, bind it tight, and tie with the purtiest knots.

There was no church on our plantation when I was a boy. All the Baptists went to Padgett's Creek, and all the Methodist went to Quaker Church and Belmont. Padget's Creek had a section in the back of the church for the slaves to sit. Quaker Church and Belmont both had slaves' galleries. There is a big book at Padgett's with three pages of slaves' names that was members. Mr. Claude Sparks read it to me last year. All the darky members dead but one. That's me.

I sure can histronize the Confederates. I come along with the Secession flag and the musterings. I careful to live at home and please the marster. In the war, I's more than careful and I stick close to him and please him, and he more than good. Us did not get mobbed up like lots of them did.

Sure, I can remember when they had the mustering grounds at the Keys. There they mustered and then they turnt in and practiced drilling them soldiers till they learnt how to march and to shoot the Yankees. When these poor white men went to the war, they left their little chillun and their wives in the hands of the darkies that was kind and the rich wives of our marsters to care for. Us took the best care of them poor white that us could under the circumstances that prevailed.

I'll say it slow so that you can catch it. I start in time of the Confederate War. With dirt dug up out of the smokehouse, water was run through it so us could get salt for bread. Hickory wood ashes was used for soda. If we didn't have no hickory wood, we burnt red corn cobs; and the ashes from them we used for cooking soda.

Molasses was made from watermelons in time of the war. They was also made from May apples or May pops, as some call them, and sometimes they was made from persimmons and from wheat bran. Simmons and wheat bran are mashed up together and baked in water, let set twenty and four hours, and cook down to molasses.

In Confederate days, Irish potato tops was cooked for vegetables. Blackberry leaves was occasionally used for greens or for seasoning lambs' quarters.

They signed me to go to the Sixteenth Regiment, but I never reached the North. When us got to Charleston, us turnt around and the bosses fetched us right back to Union through Columbia. Us heard that Sherman was coming, fetching fire along behind him.

We was sent to Sullivan's Island, but before we reached it, the Yankees done got it and we won't allowed to cross in '64. But just the same, we was in service till they give Captain Franklin Bailey permission to fetch us home. There we had to git permission for everything, just as us niggers had to get permission to leave our marster's place at home in Union County. Captain Bailey come on back to

Cross Keys with us under his protection, and we was under it for the longest time after we done got home.

All my life I is stayed in the fur end of Union County where it borders Laurens, with the Enoree dividing the two counties. It is right there that I is plowed and hoed and raised my crops for the past seventy-five years. I get money for plaiting galluses and making boot strings and other little things. Always first, I desires to be well qualified with what I does.

In Union County is where I was born and raised, and it's where I is going to be buried. Ain't never left the county but once in my life, and if the Lord see fitten, I ain't going to leave it no more, 'cept to reach the Promise Land. Lord, Lord, the Promise Land, that's where I is going when I leaves Union County.

♦ ♦ ♦

Adeline Grey

*Age 82, when interviewed by
Phoebe Faucette, in Luray, S.C.*

I REMEMBER WHEN THE Yankees come through. I was right to the old boss' place. It was on the river side. Miss Jane Warner, she was the missus. My ma used to belong to Old Man Dave Warner. I remember how she used to wash and iron and cook for the white folks during slavery time. The place here now, where all the chillun raise. Mr. Rhodes got a turpentine still there now, just after you pass the house.

I remember when my ma saw the Yankees coming that morning. She grab the sweet potatoes that been in that oven and throw 'em in the barrel of feathers that stayed by the kitchen fireplace. Just a barrel to hold chicken feathers when you pick 'em. That's all we had to eat that day.

They went into the company room where the old missus was staying and start tearing up the bed. Then, the captain come and the old missus say to him, "Please don't let them tear up my bed," and the captain went in there and tell them, "come out!"

The old missus wasn't scared. But young Miss May was sure scared. She was courting at the time. She went off and shut herself up in a room. The old

172

missus ask the captain, "Please go in and talk to the missus, she so scared." So he went in and soon he bring her out.

We chillun wasn't scared. But my brother run under the house. The soldiers went under there a-poking the bayonets into the ground to try to find where the silver buried, and they ran across him. "What you doing under here?" they say.

"I's just running the chickens out, sir," he say.

"Well, you can go on out," they say. "We ain't going to hurt you."

They choked my ma. They went to her and they say, "Where is all the white people's gold and silver?" My ma say she don't know.

"You does know," they say, and choke her till she couldn't talk.

I remember she had a red striped shawl. One of the Yankees take that and start to put it under his saddle for a saddle cloth. My brother go up to him and say, "Please sir, don't carry my ma's shawl. That the only one she got." So, he give it back to him.

They burn the ginhouse, the shop, the buggyhouse, the turkeyhouse, and the fowlhouse. Start to set the cornhouse a fire, but my ma say, "Please sir, don't burn the cornhouse. Give it to me and my chillun." So, they put the fire out. I don't know why they didn't burn the house. Must have been 'cause the captain was along. The house there now. One of the chimney down. I don't think they ever put it up again. Colored folks are in it now.

I remember when they started to break down the smokehouse door, and Old Missus come out and say, "Please don't break the door open; I got the key." So they quit.

I remember when they shoot down the hog. I

remember when they shoot the two geese in the yard. I remember when they kill the hog and cook 'em. Cook on the fire, where the little shop been. Cook 'em and eat 'em. Why didn't they cook 'em on the stove in the house? Didn't have no stoves. Just had to cook on the fireplace. Had an oven to fit in the fireplace.

Old Missus had give my ma a good moss mattress. But the Yankees had carry that off. Rip it up, throw out the moss, and put meat in it. Fill it full of meat. Them Yankees put the meat in the sack and go on off. It was late then, about dusk. I remember how the missus bring us all round the fire. It was dark then.

"Well chillun," she say, "I is sorry to tell you, but the Yankees has carry off your ma. I don't know if you'll ever see her anymore."

Then, we chillun all start crying. We still a-sitting there when my ma come back. She say she slip behind, and slip behind, and slip behind, and when she come to a little pine thicket by the side of the road, she dart into it, drop the sack of meat they had her carrying, and start out for home. When we had all make over her, we say to her then, "Well, why didn't you bring the sack of meat along with you?"

They took the top off Old Marster John carriage, put meat in it, and made him pull it same as a horse. Carry him way down to Lawtonville, had to pull it through the branch and all. Got the rockaway back, though—and the old man. I remember that well.

Had to mend up the old rockaway. And it made the old man sick. He keep on sick, sick, until he died. I remember how he'd say, "Don't you all worry." And he'd go out in the orchard. They'd say, "Don't bother him. Just let him be. He want to pray." After a while he died and they buried him. His name was John Stafford. They marster wasn't there. I guess he was off to the war.

I was a girl when Freedom was declared, and I can remember about the times. But, after Freedom, was the time when they suffered more than before. These chillun don't know how they blessed. To keep warm at night, they had to mak their pallet down by the fire. When all wood burn out, put on another piece. Didn't have nothing on the bed to sleep on.

My ma cooked for the white folks for one year after Freedom. I remember they cook bread, and they ain't have nothing to eat on it. Was thankful for a cornbread hoecake baked in the fireplace.

But they had some things. Had buried some meat, and some syrup. And they had some corn. My ma had saved the cornhouse. The rice burn up in the ginhouse.

I remember when the old missus used to have to make soap, out of these red oaks. Burn the wood, and catches the ashes. Put the ashes in a barrel with a trough under it, and pour the water through the ashes. If the lyewater that come out could cut a feather, it was strong.

Used to weave cloth after Freedom. Used to give a broach [a measurement of yarn] or two to weave at night. I's sometimes thread the needle for my ma, or pick the seed out the cotton, and make it into rolls to spin. Sometimes I'd work the foot pedal for my ma. Then they'd warp the thread.

If she want to dye it, she'd get indigo—you know that bush—and boil it. It was kinder blue. It would make good cloth. Sometimes, the cloth was kinder striped, one stripe of white, and one of blue. I remember how they'd warp the thread across the yarn after it was dyed, and I remember seeing my ma throw that shuttle through and weave that cloth.

I never did know my pa. He was sold off to Texas when I was young. My mother would say, "Well, chillun, you ain't never known your pa. Joe Smart carry him off to Texas when he went. I don't guess you'll ever see him."

My father was named Charles Smart. He never did come back. Joe Smart come back once, and say that our father is dead. He say our pa had three horses and he want one of them to be sent to us children here, but no arrangements had been made to get it to us. You see, he had chillun out there, too.

After Freedom, my ma plow many a day, same as a man, for us chillun. She work for Old Man Bill Mars. Then, she marry again. Part of the time they work for Mr. Benny Lawton, the one-arm man, what lost his arm in the war. These chillun don't know what hard times is. They don't know how to 'preciate our blessings.

Sarah Poindexter

Age 87, when interviewed by
Stiles M. Scruggs,
at 800 Lady Street, Columbia, S.C.

I WAS BORN IN 1850, on the plantation of Jacob Poindexter, about ten miles beyond Lexington Courthouse.

The first time I see Columbia, it the powerfulest lot of big wood houses and muddy streets I ever see in my life. The Poindexter wagon, that carry my daddy, my mammy, and me to the big town, pretty often mire in mudholes all along the big road from the plantation to the courthouse. That trip was made about 1857, 'cause I was seven years old when I made that trip.

Since that first trip, I has lived in sight of Columbia, most all my life. My daddy, my mammy, and me lived on the plantation of Marster Poindexter until 1863. We might a-lived there longer, if things had not been so upset. I sure recall the excitement in the neighborhood, when roving crowds of niggers come along the big road, shouting and singing that all the niggers am free. Snow was on the ground, but the spirits of the niggers was sure plenty hot.

The Poindexter plantation was one big place of excitement them days. The slaves work some, all during the war; sometimes I now 'spects it was for the sake of the missus. All of us loved her, 'cause she was so kind and good to us. Missus Poindexter many times fetch me a piece of candy or something when she go to town and back. She was crying and worrying all the time about her menfolks, who was away fighting damn Yankees, she say.

It seem like the war last forever to me, 'stead of about five years. To a child, Lordy, how long the years hang on, and when we get past fifty, oh, how fast the time runs.

No, I never see Columbia burn in 1865, but we reckon that it was burning that night in February 1865, 'cause we smell it and the whole east look like some extra light is shining, and pretty soon, some folks come riding by and tell us the whole city in flames. The next time I see it, I guess there wasn't fifty houses standing. Chimneys standing round is about all there was, where most of the city was standing before.

My daddy was killed down about Aiken, shortly after 1865. Me and Mammy come to Columbia and live in a cabin in the alley back of Senate Street, where Mammy take in washing and cook for some white folks who know her. I helped her. She die in 1868, and I goes away with four other nigger gals to Durham to work in a tobacco factory. Both white and nigger women work there, but the nigger women do most of the hard work—stripping the leaves, stemming them, and placing them to dry. White women finish them for the trade.

In 1870, when I comes back to Columbia, the city am a-coming back. Big buildings up along the streets, but most of them was made of wood. Soon after that I gets work in a hotel, but Columbia at that time was not so big, and Durham was smaller still, although Durham had more brick houses. I was happier on the Poindexter plantation and had fewer things to worry about than when I was a-scratching around for myself.

Yes, I marry a dandy-looking young man, about my own age, about a year after I comes back to Columbia. His name, so he say, is Sam Allen. He make fun of some other niggers who work at one thing or another to live. One day he come to where I work and say he bound to raise ten dollars. I hands him the cash, and he gives me a good kiss right there before the folks, but I never see him again. I hear, after he gone, that he win some more money at a gambling place on Assembly Street, and reckon he decided to blow away, while blowing was good.

The folks who know me always call me Sarah Poindexter. I got it honestly, like other honest slaves who never know what their real name was, and so, I keeps it to the end of the road.

Peter Clifton

Age 89, when interviewed by
W. W. Dixon, in Winnsboro, S.C.

Y ES, SIR, US HAD a bold, driving, pushing marster, but not a hard-hearted one. I sorry when military come and arrest him.

It was this-a-way: Him try to carry on with free labor, about like him did in slavery.

Old Marster went to the field and cuss a nigger woman for the way she was working, chopping cotton. She turnt on him with the hoe and gashed him about the head with it. Him pull out his pistol and shot her. Dr. Babcock say the wound in the woman not serious. Chester was in military District No. 2. The whole state was under that military government. They swore out a warrant for Marster Biggers, arrest him with a squad, and take him to Charleston, where him had nigger jailors, and was kicked and cuffed about like a dog. They say the only thing he had to eat was cornmeal mush brought round to him and other nice white folks in a tub, and it was ladled out to them through the iron railing in the palms of their hands.

Missus stuck by him, went and stayed down there. Missus say one time they threatened her down there, that if she didn't get up ten thousand dollars they would send him where she would never see him again. The filthy prison and hard treatments broke him down. When he did get out and come home, him passed over the river of Jordan, where I hopes and prays his soul finds rest.

That was on the Biggers Mobley place, between Kershaw and Camden, where I was born, in 1848.

My marster's first wife, I heard him say, was Missus Gilmore. There was two chillun by her. Marster Ed, that live in a palace that last time I visit Rock Hill and go to remember myself to him. Then there was Miss Mary that marry her cousin, Dr. Jim Mobley. They had one child, Captain Fred, that took the Catawba Rifles to Cuba and whip Spain for blowing up the *Maine*.

Well, Marster Biggers had a big plantation and a big mansion four miles southeast of Chester. He buy my mammy and her chillun in front of the courthouse door in Chester, at the sale of the Clifton estate. Then, he turn around and buy my pappy there, 'cause my mammy and sister Lizzie was crying about him have to leave them. Mind you I wasn't born then. Marster Biggers was a widower then and went down and courted the Widow Gibson, who had a plantation and fifty slaves between Kershaw and Camden. There is where I was born.

Marster had one child, a boy, by my missus, Miss Sallie. They call him Black George. Him live long enough to marry a angel, Miss Kate McCrorey. They had four chillun. There got to be ninety slaves on the place before war come on. One time I go with pappy to the Chester place. Seem like more slaves there than on the Gibson place. Us was fed up to the neck all the time, though us never had a change of clothes. Us smell pretty rancid maybe, in the wintertime, but in the summer us not wear very much. Girls had a slip on and the boys happy in their shirt tails.

My pappy name Ned; my mammy name Jane. My brothers and sisters was Tom, Lizzie, Mary, and Gill. Us live in a log house with a plank floor and a wooden chimney, that was always catching a fire and the wind coming through and filling the room with smoke and cinders. It was just one of many others, just like it, that made up the quarters. Us had peg beds for the old folks and just pallets on the floor for the chillun. Mattresses was made of wheat straw, but the pillows on the bed was cotton. I does remember that Mammy had a chicken feather pillow she made from the feathers she saved at the kitchen.

The rule on the place was: Wake up the slaves at daylight, begin work when they can see, and quit work when they can't see. But they was careful of the rule that say: You mustn't work a child, under twelve years old, in the field.

Kept foxhounds on both places. Old Butler was the squirrel and possum dog. Marster, there is nothing better than possum and yellow sweet taters. Right now, I wouldn't turn that down for pound cake and Delaware grape wine, like my missus used to eat and sip while she watch my mammy and Old Aunt Tilda run the spinning wheels.

Marster Biggers believe in whipping and working his slaves long and hard; then a man was scared all the time of being sold away from his wife and chillun. They put the foots in a stock and clamp them together, then they have a crosspiece go right across the breast high as the shoulder. That crosspiece long enough to bind the hands of a slave to it at each end. They always strip them naked and some time they lay on the lashes with a whip, a switch, or a strap.

I see Marster buy many a slave. I never saw him sell but one, and he sold that one to a drover for $450, cash down on the table, and he did that at the request of the overseer and the missus. They was uneasy about him (the slave).

Us always have a dance in the Christmas. They give us Christmas Day. Every woman got a handkerchief to tie up her hair. Every girl got a ribbon, every boy a Barlow knife, and every man a shinplaster [refers to paper money of the time, usually devalued].

After Freedom, when us was told us had to have names, Pappy say he love his old marster Ben Clifton the best and him took that titlement, and I's been a Clifton ever since.

You ask me what for I seek out Christina for to marry. There was something about that gal, that day I meets her, though her hair had about a pound of cotton thread in it, that just attracted me to her like a fly will sail round and light on a molasses pitcher. I kept the Ashford Ferry road hot till I got her. I had to ask her old folks for her before she consent. Her have been a blessing to me every day since.

Isiah Jefferies

Age 86, when interviewed by
Caldwell Sims, in Gaffney, S.C.; August 1937.

I IS WHAT IS known as a outside child. I lived on
the Jefferies plantation, below Wilkinsville in
Cherokee County. My mother was Jane Jefferies.
She was sold in slavery to Henry Jefferies. My
father was Henry Jefferies. My mother had three
outside chilluns, and we each had a different father.

Marster and Missus had six chilluns. Her name
was Ellen and her house was three stories high.
Their overseers always lived with them. There was
a lot of slaves, and they all loved the white folks.
The whole plantation was always up at sunup. But
we did not work very late. I remember the patrollers, the Ku Klux, and the Yankees. Niggers dreaded
all three. There was no jail for us: The patrollers
kept us straight.

First thing I had to do as a child was to mind my
ma's other chilluns, as I was the first outside one
that she had. This I did until I was about twelve
years old.

Ma teached me how to cook before I was twelve
years old. We had good things to eat then; more
than my chilluns has these times. All the slaves had
their gardens on my marster's plantation. He made
them do it, and they liked it. Niggers do not seem

to take no pains with gardens now. Land ain't soft and mellow like it used to be. In cold weather, we had to bank out taters, rutabagas, beets, carrots, and pumpkins. The pumpkins and carrots was for the hogs and cows.

In warm weather we had cotton clothes, and in cold weather we had woolen clothes that our marster had made for us by the old ladies on the plantation. But we did go barefooted all winter until we was grown and married. We had all the wood we wanted for fire. We kept fire all day and all night. We sat by the fire in winter and popped corn, parched pinders [peanuts], and roasted corn ears.

My mother's husband was named Ned. Before her marriage, she was a Davis. I always lived with my mother, and Ned was as good to me as he was to his own chillun. After she married Ned, then he jest come to be our pa—that is, he let her give us his name. She and Ned had four chillun.

My ma and Ned was working one day and I was minding her chilluns as usual, when I looked up and seed the top of our house on fire. I hollered, and they come running from the field. The other hands come with them, 'cause I made such a noise hollering. Soon, the big folks got the fire out. After that, Marster Henry had me to leave the house and go to work for him.

It was spring, and I started in chopping cotton. Appears that I got on pretty well, and that the overseer liked me from the start. From there on, I was broke into field work of all kinds, and then I did work around the lot, as well. It was not long before everybody started calling me Uncle Zery— why, I did not know, but anyway, that name still sticks to me by them that knows me well.

My grandpa never called me that, 'cause I was

named after him and he too proud of that fact to call me any nickname. I stayed with him at his house lots after I started working for the marster, 'cause he showed me how to do things. I worked for him to get my first money, and he would give me a quarter for a whole day's work. That made me feel good, and I thought I was a man 'cause I made a quarter.

In them days, a quarter was a lot of money. I spent it for chewing tobacco, and that made me sick at first. That's all men had to spend money for in them days. Everything was give you on the plantation, and you did not need much money. Sometimes we cooked out in the field, and I have cooked bread in the field in a lid.

When I got to be a big boy, my ma got religion at the camp meeting at El-Bethel. She shouted and sung for three days, going all over the plantation and the neighboring ones, inviting her friends to come to see her baptized, and shouting and praying for them.

She went around to all the people that she had done wrong and begged their forgiveness. She sent for them that had wronged her and told them that she was born again and a new woman, and that she would forgive them. She wanted everybody that was not saved to go up with her.

The white folks was baptized in the pool first, and then their darkies. When the darkies' time come, they sung and shouted so loud that the patrollers come from somewhere, but Marster and Missus made them go away and let us shout and rejoice to the fullest.

Missus had all her darkies that was a-going in for baptizing to wear white calico in the pool. In the sewing room, she had had calico robes made for everybody. My ma took me with her to see her baptized, and I was so happy that I sung and shouted with her. All the niggers joined in singing. The white folks stayed and saw us baptize our folks, and they liked our singing.

My first wife is dead and my second wife is named Alice Jefferies. I got one child by my first wife, and I ain't got no outside chilluns. That works out bad, at best. None of my folks is living. All of them is done dead now. Just me, my wife, and my sister's daughter, Emma, who is grown now. Her pa and her ma took and went crazy before they died. Both of them died in the asylum. We took Emma, and she ain't just exactly right; but she ain't no bother to us.

Robert Toatley

Age 82, when interviewed by
W. W. Dixon, near White Oak, S.C.

I WAS BORN ON the Elizabeth Mobley place. Us always called it Cedar Shades. There was a half-mile of cedars on both sides of the road leading to the fine house that our white folks lived in.

My marster was rich. Slaves lived in quarters, three hundred yards from the big house. A street run through the quarters, homes on each side. Beds was homemade. Mattresses made of wheat straw. Bed covers was quilts and counterpanes, all made by slave women.

Never had any money, didn't know what it was. Mammy was a housewoman, and I got just what the white chillun got to eat, only a little bit later, in the kitchen. There was fifty or sixty other little niggers on the place. Want to know how they was fed? Well, it was like this: You've seen pig troughs, side by side, in a big lot? After all the grown niggers eat and get out the way, scraps and everything eatable was put in them troughs. Sometimes buttermilk poured on the mess and sometimes potlicker. Then, the cook blowed a cow horn. Quick as lightning a passel of fifty or sixty little niggers run out the plum bushes, from under the sheds and houses, and from everywhere. Each one take his place and souse his hands in the mixture and eat just like you see pigs shoving around slop troughs.

The biggest whipping I ever heard tell of was when they had a trial of several slave men for selling liquor at the spring, during preaching, on Sunday. The trial come off at the church about a month later. They was convicted, and the order of the court was: Edmund to receive 100 lashes, Sam and Andy each 125 lashes, and Frank and Abram 75 lashes. All to be given on their bare backs and rumps, well laid on with strap. If the courts would sentence like that these days, there'd be more attention to the law.

My white folks, the Mobleys, made us work on Sunday sometime, with the fodder, and when the plowing get behind. They mighty neighborly to rich neighbors but didn't have much time for poor buckra. I tell you, poor white men have poor chance to rise, make something and be something, before the old war. Some of these same poor buckra done had a chance since then and they way up in G [government] now. They mighty nigh run the county and town of Winnsboro, plum mighty nigh it, I tell you.

My missus was a daughter of Dr. John Glover. When her oldest child, Sam, come back from college, he fetched a classmate, Jim Carlisle, with him. That boy, Jini, made his mark, got religion, and went to the top of a college in Spartanburg. Marster Sam study to be a doctor. He start to practice, and then he marry Miss Lizzie Rice down in Barnwell. Missus give me to them, and I went with them and stayed till Freedom.

'Twas not till the year of '66 that we got reliable information and felt free to go where us pleased to go. Most of the niggers left, but Mammy stayed on and cooked for Dr. Sam and the white folks.

Bad white folks comed and got bad niggers started. Soon, things got wrong and the devil took a hand in the mess. Out of it come to the top the carpetbag, the scalawags, and then the Ku Klux. Night rider come by and drop something at your door and say, "I'll just leave you something for dinner." Then ride off in a gallop. When you open the sack, what you reckon in there? One time it was six nigger heads that was left at the door.

Was it at my house door? Oh, no! It was at the door of a nigger too active in politics. Old Congressman Wallace sent Yankee troops, three miles long, down here. Lots of white folks was put in jail.

I married Emma Greer in 1870; she been dead two years. Us lived husband and wife fifty-six years, bless God. Us raised ten chillun; all is going well. All us Presbyterians. Can read, but can't write. Our slaves was told if ever they learned to write, they'd lose the hand or arm they wrote with.

Sylvia Cannon

*Age 85, when interviewed by
Annie Ruth Davis, at Marion Street,
Florence S.C.; October 1937.*

I DON'T KNOW EXACTLY how old I is 'cause the
peoples used to wouldn't tell they chillun how
old they was before they was grown. There been
about fourteen head of we chillun, and they all
gone but me. I the last one.

Yes, ma'am, I been a little small girl in slavery
time. I just can remember when I was sold. Me and
Becky and George. Just can remember that, but I
know who bought me. First belong to the old Bill
Greggs, and that where Miss Earlie Hatchel bought
me from. Never did know where Becky and George
went.

I see 'em sell plenty colored peoples away in them
days, 'cause that the way white folks made heap of
they money. Course, they ain't never tell us how
much they sell 'em for. Just stand 'em up on a block
about three feet high and a speculator bid 'em off
just like they was horses. Them what was bid of
didn't never say nothing neither. Don't know who
bought my brothers, George and Earl.

I see 'em sell some slaves twice before I was sold,
and I see the slaves when they be traveling like hogs
to Darlington. Some of them be women folks looking like they going to get down, they so heavy.

Yes, ma'am, the Bill Greggs had a heap of slaves 'cause they had my grandmammy and my granddaddy and they had a heap of chillun. My mammy, she belong to the Greggs, too. She been Mr. Greggs's cook, and I the one name ater her. I remembers she didn't talk much to we chillun. Mostly, she did sing about all the time.

> Oh Heaven, sweet Heaven,
> When shall I see?
> If you get there before me,
> You tell my Lord I on the way.

Oh, that be a old song what my grandmammy used to sing way back there.

The white folks didn't never help none of we black people to read and write no time. They learn the yellow chillun, but if they catch we black chillun with a book, they nearly 'bout kill us. They was sure better to them yellow chillun than the black chillun that be on the plantation. Northern women come there after the war, but they didn't let 'em teach nobody nothing.

Father and Mother belong to the old Bill Greggs and that where Miss Earlie Hatchel buy me from. After that, I didn't never live with my parents anymore, but I went back to see them every two weeks. Got a note and go on a Sunday evening and come back to Miss Hatchel on Monday. Miss Hatchel want a nurse and that howcome she buy me.

I remembers Miss Hatchel putting the baby in my lap and tell me don't drop him. Didn't have to do no work much in them days, but they didn't allow me to play none neither. When the baby sleep, I sweep the yard, work the garden, and pick seed out the cotton to spin. Oh, honey, there won't no such thing as cotton mill, train, sawmill, or nothing like that in my day. People had to sit there at night and pick the seed out the cotton with they own hands.

We lived in the quarter about one-half mile from the white folks' house in a one-room pole house what was daubed with dirt. There was about twenty other colored people house there in the quarter. The ground been us floor and us fireplace been down on the ground. Take sticks and make chimney, 'cause there won't no bricks and won't no sawmills to make lumber when I come along.

Oh, my white folks live in a pole house daubed with dirt, too. Us just had some kind of homemade bedstead with pine straw bed what to sleep on in them days. Sew croaker [burlap] sack together and stuff 'em with pine straw. That how they make they mattress.

Didn't get much clothes to wear in that day and time neither. Man never wear no breeches in the summer. Go in his shirttail that come down to the knees and a woman been glad enough to get one-piece homespun frock what was made with they hand. Make petticoat out of old dress and patch and patch till couldn't tell which place weave. Always put wash out on a Saturday night and dry it and put it back on Sunday. Then get oak leaves and make a hat what to wear to church.

I go to church with my white folks, but they never have no church like they have these days. The bush was they shelter, and when it rain, they meet 'round from one house to another. Ride to church in the ox cart, 'cause I had to carry the baby everywhere I go. White folks didn't have no horse then.

Marster and Missus taught me to say a prayer that go like this:

The angels in Heaven love us,
Bless Mamma and bless Papa,
Bless our Missus,
Bless the man that feeding us,
For Christ sake.

We didn't never have but one pair of shoes a
year, and they was these here brogans with thick
soles and brass toes. Had shop there on the plantation where white man made all the shoes and plows.
They would save all the cowhide and soak it in salt
two or three weeks to get the hair off it. They have
big trough ewed out where they clean it after they
get the hair off it. After that, it was turn to the man
at the shop.

Oh, yes, they have white overseers then. I hear
some people say they was good people. At night the
overseer would walk out to see could he catch any
of us walking without a note, and to this day, I
don't want to go nowhere without a paper.

It just like this: The overseer didn't have to be
right behind you to see that you work in them days.
They have all the fields named and the overseer just
had to call on the horn and tell you what field to go
work in that day. Then, he come along on a Saturday evening to see what you done.

Yes, ma'am, white folks had to whip some of they
niggers in slavery time; they be so mean. Some was
mean 'cause they tell stories on one another and been
swear to it. My mammy tell me don't never tell
nothing but the truth and I won't get no whipping.

I remembers when night come on and we go back
to the quarter, we cook bread in the ashes and pick
seed from the cotton. My mama sat there and sew
heap of the time. Then, I see 'em when they have
them hay pullings. They tote torch to gather the hay

by. After they pull two or three stacks of hay, they
have a big supper, dance in the road, beat sticks, and
blow cane. Had to strike fire on cotton with two
rocks, 'cause they didn't have no match in them days.

We fare good in that day and time. They never
whip me in all my life. Tell me if I don't know how
to do anything to tell them, and they show me how.
I remembers Miss Hatchel caught and shook me
one time, and when I tell her husband he tell her to
keep her hands off his little nigger. They all was
good to me. When I start home to see my mama,
they cry after me till I come back.

Folks eat all kind of things during the war. Eat
honeysuckle off the low sweet bush after the flower
falls off and pine nuts that they get out the burr and
sour weeds. Wouldn't nobody eat them things these
days. Course, they let the slaves have three acres of
land to a family to plant for they garden. Work
them in moonlight nights and on a Saturday evening.

I telling you my missus sure was good to me in
that day and time. She been so good to me that I
stay there with her twenty year after I got free. Stay
there till I marry the old man Isenia Cannon. You
see my old marster got killed in the war. She tell me
I better stay where I can get flour bread to eat,
'cause she make her own flour and bake plenty
biscuit in the oven. Then, she kill hogs and a cow
every Christmas and give us all the eggnog and
liquor we want that day. Dig hole in the ground and
roast cow over log fire.

When I get hard up for meat and couldn't get
nothing else, I catch rabbits and birds. Make a
death trap with a lid, bait it with cabbage and corn,
and catch them that way. Then another time, I dig
deep hole in the ground and daub it with clay and
fill it up with water. Rabbits hunt water in the

night, fall in there, and drown. I used to set traps heap of times to keep the rabbits from eating up the people gardens.

My son born in the year of the earthquake [1886], and if he had lived, I would been blessed with plenty grandchillun these days. I remember all about the shake. They tell me one man, Mr. Turner, give away his dog two or three days before the earthquake come on. That dog get loose and come back the night of the shake.

Come back with chain tied round his neck, and Mr. Turner been scared most to death, so they tell me. He say, "Oh, Mr. Devil, don't put the chain on me, I'll go with you." That was his dog come back and he thought it was the devil come there to put the chain on him.

Didn't hear tell about no telephone nowhere in them days, and people never live no closer than three and four miles apart neither. Got Old Marster horn right in that room there now that he could talk on to people that be sixteen miles from where he was. Come in here, child, and I'll let you see it.

See, this old horn been made out of silver money. You talks in that little end and what you say runs out that big end. Man ask me didn't I want to sell it, and I tell him I ain't got no mind to get rid of it 'cause it been belong to Old Marster. Then, if I get sick, I call on it and somebody come. I sold Old Marster's sword last week for ten cents, but I ain't going do away with his old horn. It the old-time phone. Got Old Marster's maul, too, and this here Grandpa oxen bit that was made at home.

The peoples use herb medicines that they get out the woods for they cures in them days. I make a herb medicine that good for anything. Couldn't tell you how I make it 'cause that would ruin me. Town people try to buy the remedy from me, but Dr. McLeod tell me not to sell it.

Times was sure better long time ago than they be now. I know it. Colored people never had no debt to pay in slavery time. Never hear tell about no colored people been put in jail before Freedom. Had more to eat and more to wear then, and had good clothes all the time 'cause white folks furnish everything, everything. Had plenty peas, rice, hog meat, rabbit, fish, and such as that.

Had they extra crop what they had time off to work every Saturday. White folks tell them: What they made, they could have. Peoples would have found we colored people rich with the money we made on the extra crop, if the slaves hadn't never been set free. Us had big rolls of money, and then when the Yankees come and change the money, that what made us poor.

It let the white people down and let us down, too. Left us all to about starve to death. Been force to go to the fish pond and the huckleberry patch. Land went down to a dollar a acre. White people let us clear up new land and make us own money that way. We bury it in the ground and that howcome I had money. I dig mine up one day and had over fifteen hundred dollars that I been save. People back there didn't spend money like they do these days and that howcome I had that money. They would just spend money once a year in that day and time.

Rich man up there in Florence learn about I was worth over fifteen hundred dollars, and he tell me that I ought to buy a house, that I was getting old. Say he had a nice place he want to sell me. He say, "Mom Sylvia, you stay here long as you live, 'cause you ain't going be here much longer."

Yes, ma'am, I pay that man over nine hundred

dollars. Been paying on it long time and got it all paid but $187 and city find out what that man had done. I thought this house been belong to me, but they tell me this here place be city property. I been trust white folks and he take my money and settle me down here on city property.

City tell me just stay on right here, but don't pay no more money out. I beg the town to let me go out to the poor farm and stay, but they say I done pay too much to move. Tell me stay on here and keep the house up the best way I can. They give me that garden and tell me what I make I can have.

I promise my God right then not to save no more money, child. If the town picks up any sick person, they bring them here and tell me do the best I can for them. City tell me do like I was raised and so I been chopping here about twenty years.

I ain't able to do no kind of work much. No more than chopping my garden. Can't hardly see nothing on a sunny day. I raise my own seed all right, 'cause sometimes I can't see and find myself is cut up things, and that make me has to plant over another time.

The peoples sure been blessed with more religion in them days than these days. Didn't never have to look up nothing then, and if you tell a story, you get a whipping. Now, the peoples tell me to tell a story. I been cleaning up a lady porch and she tell me to tell anybody what come there that she ain't home.

A lady come and ask for her, and I tell her, "she say anybody come here, tell 'em 'I ain't home.' If you don't believe she here, look in the bedroom."

Miss Willcox come out there and beat me in the back. I tell her, "Don't read the Bible and tell me to tell a story. I ain't going tell no story, 'cause my white folks learnt me not to do that."

Savilla Burrell

Age 83, when interviewed by
W. W. Dixon, in Winnsboro, S.C.

M Y MARSTER IN SLAVERY time was Captain Tom
Still. He had big plantation down there on Jackson Creek. My missus's name was Mary Ann, though she wasn't his first wife—just a second wife, and a widow when she captivated him. You know widows is like that anyhow, 'cause they done had experience with mens and wraps them round their little finger and get them under their thumb before the mens knows what going on. Young gals have a poor chance against a young widow like Miss Mary Ann was. Her had her troubles with Marster Tom after her get him, I tell you, but maybe best not to tell that, right now anyways.

Marster Tom had four chillun by his first wife. They was John, Sam, Henrietta, and I can't remember the name of the other one, least right now. They teached me to call chillun three years old Young Marster, and say Missie. They whip you if they ever hear you say Old Marster or Old Missie. That riled them.

My pappy name Sam; my mother name Mary. My pappy did not live on the same place as Mother. He was a slave of the Hamiltons, and he got a pass sometimes to come and be with her, not often.

Grandmammy name Esther, and she belonged to our marster Tom Still, too.

Us lived in a log cabin with a stick chimney. The bed was nailed to the side of the walls. Just one room.

Never seen any money. Us half-naked all the time. Grown boys went around barefooted and in their shirttail all the summer. There was plenty to eat such as it was, but in the summertime, before us get there to eat, the flies would be all over the food and some was swimming in the gravy and milk pots. Marster laughed about that and say it made us fat.

Marster was a rich man. He had a big gin house and sheep, goats, cows, mules, horses, turkeys, geese, and a stallion named Stocking-Foot. Us little niggers was scared to death of that stallion. Mothers used to say to chillun to quiet them, "Better hush, Stocking-Foot will get you and tramp you down." Any child would get quiet at that.

Old Marster was the daddy of some mulatto chillun. The relations with the mothers of those chillun is what give so much grief to Missus. The neighbors would talk about it, and he would sell all them chillun away from they mothers to a trader. My missus would cry about that. They sell one of Mother's chillun once, and when she take on and cry about it, Marster say, "Stop that sniffing there if you don't want to get a whipping." She grieve and cry at night about it.

Our doctor was old Marster's son-in-law, Dr. Martin. I seen him cup a man once. He was a good doctor. He give slaves castor oil, bleed them sometimes, and make them take pills.

Us looked for the Yankees on that place like us look now for the Savior and the host of angels at the Second Coming. They come one day in Febru-

ary. They took everything carryable off the plantation and burnt the big house, stables, barns, gin
house. They left the slave houses.

After the war, I marry Osborne Burrell and live
on the Tom Jordan place. I's the mother of twelve
chillun. Just three living now. I lives with the Mills
family three miles above town. My son Willie got
killed at the DuPont Powder Plant at Hopewell,
Virginia, during the World War.

Young Marster Sam Still got killed in the Civil
War. Old Marster live on. I went to see him in his
last days, and I sat by him and kept the flies off
while there. I see the lines of sorrow had plowed on
that old face, and I remembered he'd been a captain on horseback in that war. It come into my
remembrance the song of Moses: "The Lord had
triumphed glorily and the horse and his rider have
been throwed into the sea."

Ⓢ

Recommended Reading from SIGNET

There's an epidemic with 27 million victims. And no visible symptoms.

It's an epidemic of people who can't read.

Believe it or not, 27 million Americans are functionally illiterate, about one adult in five.

The solution to this problem is you... when you join the fight against illiteracy. So call the Coalition for Literacy at toll-free 1-800-228-8813 and volunteer.

Volunteer Against Illiteracy.
The only degree you need is a degree of caring.